TRADE SHOW

4 1 1

the **ESSENTIAL GUIDE** to
EXHIBITING LIKE A PRO

TRADE SHOW

4 1 1

the **ESSENTIAL GUIDE** to
EXHIBITING LIKE A PRO

LISA M. MASIELLO

ISBN: 978-1-7374878-0-7 (paperback)
ISBN: 978-1-7374878-1-4 (e-book)

Printed in the United States of America.

To Linda Killion

You provided the spark that started me on this exciting, sometimes maddening, but always interesting journey.

Contents

Chapter 6: Sleep With It Under Your Pillow

Chapter 7: Don't Be the Last Horse Out of the Starting Gate

Chapter 8: Mining for Gold

Chapter 9: Everyone Needs to Row in the Same Direction

Chapter 10: Don't Play Pin the Tail on the Donkey

Chapter 11: To Own or Not to Own, That Is the Question

Chapter 12: Recognize a Great Opportunity When It Presents Itself

Chapter 13: Have Your Cake and Eat It Too

Chapter 14: The Good Publicity Hound

Chapter 15: For Immediate Release

Foreword
Patricia Hammond

Trade show marketing was a frustrating mystery until I met Lisa Masiello.

I'm enough of a dreamer to be a serial entrepreneur. I've started and grown companies as diverse as a collection agency, a web development firm, and a digital magazine.

My latest venture, The Business Guild, is the culmination of twenty-five years of experience as a business owner wearing more hats than I can count.

The reason I mention this is because I want you to understand that I am not a newbie. I've been there, done that, and usually know how to find answers.

I know that success is a combination of planning, hard work, and having the good sense to ask for help when you need it. It also requires having the right connections and luck.

A lot of luck.

That's how I met Lisa.

I'm not a fan of woo-woo ideas like the Law of Attraction that rely on wishful thinking rather than hard work, but it was difficult to ignore as it smacked me in the face and told me to pay attention.

I was still working as a web developer, ironing out the kinks for monetizing the marketing platform that eventually became The Business Guild when Lisa showed up at one of my networking groups.

She is an expert marketer, entrepreneur, and said her agency, TECHmarc Labs, specialized in technology marketing. I worked in tech, had friends with successful tech startups, and have done a lot of small business marketing, but I didn't really know what Lisa did.

Then one day over coffee, the subject of trade shows came up. I told her about how I kept hitting a dead-end in my search for specific information about using trade shows for marketing.

I knew there was more to it than setting up a table and waiting for people to come, but most of the information I found lacked substance and credibility.

How do you prepare for a trade show?

How do you budget?

How do you drive traffic to your booth?

How do you engage customers?

How do you maximize your ROI?

It turned out that trade shows were Lisa's area of expertise and her passion.

With over thirty years of experience managing regional, national, and international trade show exhibits, Lisa has encountered just about every scenario for planning and executing a trade show event.

♦ Language barriers
♦ Unexpected pillars in the middle of your booth space
♦ DIY repairs without tools
♦ Hunger and fatigue
♦ Damaged booths
♦ Missing marketing materials, and more

Trade show exhibits have the potential to bring visibility, leads, and sales to your organization, but they are a lot of work.

Anyone who wants to be a successful trade show marketing manager must be able to work in the trenches. They need to know how to manage people and activities while maintaining a budget and adapting on the fly when one or more pieces of the plan go sideways.

It's a high-pressure job that requires you to understand that anything you plan can go wrong, and anything you don't plan for will cost you money.

This is not something they teach you in school. A marketing degree will get you in the door and help you develop the plan to engage your target market, but it takes grit, determination, and a lot of experience to transform that plan into a successful trade show campaign.

That is where *Trade Show 411* shines.

Lisa has channeled her extensive marketing experience into an easy-to-read blend of anecdotes, tips, and action steps you can apply to your own trade show exhibit.

♦ Goals and strategy
♦ PR and marketing
♦ Budget management
♦ Show and booth staffing (They're not always the same.)
♦ Setup and breakdown

Whether you are a trade show novice or are looking for some insights into how to improve your trade show marketing strategy and tactics, *Trade Show 411* is must-read.

It tackles all the ins and outs of how to manage a successful trade show campaign.

It's a perfect balance of experienced insights and explanations to help you understand the mysteries and mechanics of successful trade show marketing.

Patricia Hammond
Co-founder and CEO, The Business Guild
thebizguild.com

Introduction

My very first trade show as an exhibit manager took place in Paris, France. I worked for a technology company, and I was their marketing coordinator.

On the one hand, I was terrified; it was my first trade show.

Sure, I had participated in trade shows as an attendee, but that is entirely different than managing a company's exhibit at a show.

Now I was in charge.

Presenting the public face of the company to fifteen thousand attendees was on my shoulders. I didn't tell my boss or the rest of the team that it was my very first show.

What's more, it was in a foreign country, with foreign exhibitor rules, and a foreign language. One year of high school French wasn't going to be enough.

I had to figure out how to get all our crates and boxes to Paris.

Where would I find a reputable shipping company?

How could I ensure that nothing got stuck in transit?

Imagine if airport customs officers in Paris detained our booth, and I had nothing to install at the show! I started sweating just thinking about it.

My boss decided that we didn't need to hire show labor to install and dismantle our booth. "We can do it ourselves," he said. Of course, when he said *we*, he really meant *me*. His view was that we were already traveling to one of the most expensive cities in the world, and expenses needed to be cut.

On the other hand, it was Paris!

Although I had previously traveled to Europe, I had never been to Paris. I was excited to be going to such a wonderful city. Better still, the company was going to pay all my expenses. What a great opportunity.

"Yeah, that's the ticket. Let's think of it as a great opportunity, and I might forget that I have no experience developing and implementing a trade show exhibitor strategy," I said to myself with fingers crossed.

My first mistake was thinking that we could install a booth on our own without tools or equipment.

We had a beautiful custom-built 10 x 20 ft. booth with an 8 ft. high metal truss that spanned the entire 20 ft. length of the booth. The truss was used as a design element but also to hang lights and our company's logoed banner, which was designed to hang gracefully, like a sail.

Unfortunately, we didn't have the ladders, wrenches, hammers, and other tools needed to install the booth, and we couldn't borrow them from other booth laborers. I don't know why this didn't dawn on me in the pre-show planning phase.

In the end, after hours of standing on wobbly chairs trying to put the booth together ourselves, I visited the exhibitor services desk to hire a group of French laborers to put the rest of the booth together for us.

Not only did we end up having to spend money on labor, but we also paid more than we would have if we had ordered the labor four weeks earlier before the advance order deadline expired.

My second mistake was trying to fit precut booth carpet around a convention center column that moved.

I decided it would be more cost-effective to buy carpet from our exhibit house and ship it with the booth from show to show rather than renting new carpet for each show.

That was the wrong decision on so many levels.

First, we incurred shipping costs of sending a two-hundred-pound roll of carpet from Boston, Massachusetts to Paris, France. If the flooring had been lightweight, interlocking foam blocks, it would have been fine. A two-hundred-pound roll of carpet was not lightweight.

Second, the Paris convention center floor plan showed an expo hall column located in the front left corner of our space next to the main aisle.

As a result, I asked our exhibit house to cut our carpet to the exact size, including the additional cutout, so the carpet could seamlessly wrap around the column.

When I arrived at the Paris convention center on installation day, I realized that show management had shifted all rows of booths throughout the hall one foot to the left. That meant the column initially on the outer corner of our booth space was now one foot further inside our booth space. And, since I precut the carpet to perfectly match the original floor plan dimensions, I now had a hole in my carpet where the column was supposed to be and carpet where the column was.

Because of the column's round shape, the newly cut carpet was an odd size, resulting in a hole the size of a large man's foot. It was a nightmare. What would you have done?

I contacted the show's plant vendor that rented floral arrangements, green plants, and trees. I rented a palm-type plant in a container large enough to cover the hole but not so large that it would prevent attendees from easily entering our booth. The plant was delivered during booth installation and was taken away during dismantle when the show was over, so no show attendees ever knew we had a big hole in our carpet.

◆ ◆ ◆

Although I have planned, managed, attended, and exhibited at hundreds of trade shows across the United States and in countries worldwide, they never cease to amaze me.

On the first day of setup, I walk into a hall chock-full of booths in different stages of assembly with large wooden crates, piles of trash, carpet rolls, ladders, and tools littering the aisles. People climb over shipping containers to get from one end of the hall to the other.

It's impossible to imagine how these booths will be installed, trash collected, crates removed, and the aisle carpet laid down by the time the doors open to attendees.

But, sure enough, as I enter the hall on opening day, I'm greeted with a spectacular sight—sparkling glass, bright backlit signs, gleaming countertops, spotless carpets, and lots of smiling happy faces.

Then, as soon as the show ends, it's as if the trade show genie snapped his finger and the expo hall goes back to an empty shell.

Trade show and conference attendees never see the incredible amount of planning, work, sweat, and experience needed to successfully manage a company's participation in an event that, to them, seems effortless to produce.

You and I both know that's not true.

Why I wrote this book

When I was at the beginning of my marketing career, I didn't ask questions. I didn't ask for help. I didn't want to appear as if I was inexperienced or incompetent. I thought it would be a sign of weakness. I was afraid I wouldn't get the next promotion. I was afraid that someone else who was more knowledgeable or experienced would take my job. I didn't know anyone else who managed exhibitor trade show participation, and I felt if I asked people how to do things, I would look ineffective.

I attempted to figure things out on my own. That was a bit more difficult to do in 1991 since the Web didn't exist. It took time to figure things out.

I'd make a mistake and learn from it.

Make another mistake and learn from it.

The problem with that is it takes time to learn. I had to stumble over many rocks before the road to successful trade show management became smooth and easy to travel.

So, why did I write this book?

Because I don't want you to have to travel down the long road to trade show success that I traveled.

I don't want you to have to go through the things I went through—the challenges, the worry, the embarrassment, the sleepless nights—hoping that everything would turn out okay.

I don't want you to hire show labor last minute because you thought you could install the booth yourself and you can't.

I don't want you to have a meltdown when you discover a hole in your carpet and don't know what to do next.

I want you to be able to hit the ground running.

I want you to be able to anticipate possible problems and eliminate them before something happens, like your crates not arriving at the hall on time or having to reconfigure your booth on the spot due to a leak in the convention center ceiling.

I want you to stop pulling your hair out from stress.

I want you to be successful!

How to Read This Book

I know you are busy, and the only way you will probably be able to read this book from cover to cover is if you are sitting on a beach on your summer vacation.

In that case, I advise you to put the book down and enjoy yourself. I'll still be here when you get back.

There are 1,001 things to do when you exhibit at a trade show. That's why I have decided that you should choose how to read this book.

As you can see in the Table of Contents, I focus each part of this book on a different stage of exhibitor management and each chapter on a specific topic within its respective stage. This is intentional.

I want you to be able to quickly find what you're looking for, get the answer, and move on to managing your event participation.

Are you trying to understand your lead capture options? Turn to chapter 21.

Want to know what to include in a post-show analysis report? Turn to chapter 29.

You can read the other chapters as time permits.

If you want a thorough understanding of the essential trade show exhibitor management components, read this book from cover to cover.

◆ ◆ ◆

You should never think of a trade show as simply those three or four days when you are on-site at the show.

Trade show management starts many months before a show begins and is not over until long after you have taped up your last box at the end of the show. That's why I divided this book into six individual parts.

Part 1: Trade show strategy

Before you can design your booth, capture leads, and close sales, you need to establish goals and objectives, make sure you pick the right show for your business, and set your budget. In this part, I'll lay the groundwork for you to be successful.

Part 2: Pre-show tips

Preparation for a show starts months before it actually begins. In this part, you'll discover how to get free money to offset your expenses, uncover a gold mine of potential booth visitors, hand-pick the perfect booth staff, and so much more.

Part 3: On-site tips

It's showtime! This section discusses on-site challenges like distributing food in your booth, incurring hidden drayage costs, overcoming bad manners that turn attendees off, and unleashing your lead management plan.

Part 4: Post-show tips

The show may be over, but your marketing and sales efforts must continue. Successful exhibit managers know that now is the time to convert leads to customers and calculate the actual return on this significant investment. Determining the true success of a show requires post-show follow-up and analysis.

Part 5: When your trade show gets turned upside down

What happens when your trade show is canceled, and the event organizer is uncertain about the new date? In this part, I'll reveal how you can stay on track without going insane.

Part 6: Essential terms you should know

Finally, I include essential trade show terms. This part is so important to me that I ripped it out of its typical location in the appendix and gave it its own chapter. Whether you are speaking with someone from a trade show sales department, reading the exhibitor services manual, or writing your post-show executive summary and evaluation report, you need to know what these terms mean to be successful at your job.

◆ ◆ ◆

Who is this book for?

This book is for you.

It is for the college student majoring in business management or marketing.

It is for the marketing administrator and coordinator just starting in their careers.

It is for the marketing manager who is asked to take on the added responsibility of managing their company's trade show and conference participation.

It is for the marketing director and chief marketing officer (CMO) who want to give their staff a head start by providing a deeper level of understanding and copies of this book.

It is for the small business owner who understands the importance of exhibiting but doesn't have any idea where to begin.

♦ ♦ ♦

Extra help along the way

Throughout this book, I have included targeted information that will help you be even more successful. Specific chapters contain icons so the information is easy to spot. I also included a chapter list so you can quickly find, read, and implement my recommendations.

Chapters that will save you time

As exhibit manager, you have a mountain of things to do. My goal is to help save you time and anticipate what lies ahead.

♦ **Chapter 18: Don't Waste My Time**
Coordinating On-Site Vendors

Chapters that will save you money

A trade show budget can quickly get out of control. These money-saving tips will help keep you on budget.

♦ **Chapter 5: One, Two, Three, and More** Booth and Show Passes/Badges
♦ **Chapter 7: Don't Be the Last Horse Out of the Starting Gate** Advance Pricing Deadline
♦ **Chapter 16: A Journey of 1,000 Miles Begins with the Right Shipper** Shipping Options

Chapters that give you the scoop on free stuff

Are there free opportunities and free stuff just waiting for you to claim them? YES!

Chapters that give you insider insights

I've been successfully managing trade show exhibits for decades. Here are important insider insights you won't hear from others.

◆◆◆

Get your free bonus gifts too!

My objective is to make your job easier and less stressful, so I've created bonus gifts for you to download and use over and over.

Each chapter with a corresponding free bonus gift includes the icon you see here.

Access your gifts by visiting https://www.lisamasiello.com/trade-show-411-exhibitor-tools.

This free bonus package includes four valuable resources:

Master budgeting spreadsheet

This event budget and cost breakdown spreadsheet will help you keep track of your expenses and quickly see whether you are under, at, or over budget.

Master staffing spreadsheet

This master staffing document helps you manage your team, confirm they have the resources they need, and are ready to represent your company at the show.

Master trade show schedule

This master schedule of pre-show, on-site, and post-show action items will help you stay on track. The worksheet includes a twelve-month, nine-month, six-month, and three-month exhibitor planning schedule to ensure you are organized no matter how much—or how little—time you have to prepare.

Master list of trade show questions

This list of trade show sales questions provides you with the foundation to determine if a particular show will help you achieve your business goals, get the most from your exhibitor experience, and whether you should exhibit or not.

◆ ◆ ◆

If I'd only known earlier

Each chapter of this book begins with a short section titled *If I'd only known earlier*. It includes an experience I had, a challenge I overcame, a lesson learned, or a tidbit of information that is important for you to know.

If I'd only known then what I know now, I would have done some things differently or would have been able to eliminate a hurdle I had to overcome. I share these pieces of information with you so you can have a head start on your journey to exhibitor success.

◆◆◆

Terminology

Although I frequently use the terms trade show and convention center throughout this book, I realize you may use other terms. Maybe you refer to an event as a conference, convention, or meeting at an expo center, hotel ballroom, or conference center.

The difference between these words is commonly an indication of the facility's physical size, the number of people they can accommodate, and whether they simply hold meetings or can run meetings and an expo at the same time.

For this book, don't get hung up on the terminology. No matter your company, location, or event size, you will be able to take advantage of the strategies and tactics I discuss.

◆◆◆

Let's get started!

Part 1
Trade Show Strategy

Chapter 1: Remind Me Why We're Doing This

insider insight

Exhibitor Goals and Objectives

If I'd only known earlier

As you begin to plan for trade show participation, I am assuming that you already completed a couple of very important tasks.

1. That you sat with your executive management team to discuss your company's goals for the coming quarter and year.

2. That you decided that using a portion of your marketing budget on live, in-person events is a beneficial strategy to help grow your company in ways that are most important to you.

Your goal as an exhibitor should be to achieve your company's business goals. It should be the very first item on your exhibitor checklist of things to do.

We will use Part 1 of this book to look at the big picture—your overall trade show strategy.

Exhibiting at a trade show without goals or objectives is like going on a trip with no GPS or pretravel planning. You'll probably get there in the end, but it will cost you more than you expect, take longer than you expect, and you won't get as much out of your experience as if you had set specific objectives for what you want to see and do. The same is true when exhibiting at a trade show.

What is the reason you plan to exhibit? Common reasons to exhibit at a trade show include:

♦ Speaking directly with potential customers
♦ Taking the opportunity to meet current customers in person
♦ Generating new sales leads
♦ Increasing awareness of your company and products among potential customers and business partners
♦ Scoping out your competition
♦ Researching a new industry you may want to target
♦ Launching a new product or service
♦ Expanding into a new market
♦ Identifying new suppliers to resell your product or vendors whose products you can resell
♦ Networking with industry influencers
♦ Looking for new employees

Determine your exhibitor goals

I'm sure you could develop a list of ten exhibitor goals for the coming year, the next six months, or the next quarter, based on your company's business goals. However, to be most effective, you should have no more than two goals for a single event. You will be able to narrow down the most appropriate trade shows to participate in based on those very specific goals.

Suppose your company's goal is to sell your products or services in a new industry like manufacturing, aerospace, healthcare, retail, financial services, legal, education, transportation, or another, and you want to generate new qualified leads from buyers in that industry. You should seek out a trade show that attracts attendees who are focused solely on that industry.

An industry association often runs this type of show.

For example, if your company is interested in selling software to healthcare providers, hospitals, doctor's offices, insurance companies, or other health-related organizations, the Healthcare Information and Management Systems Society (HIMSS) conference should be at the top of your list. The HIMSS runs this conference, and exhibitors have access to forty-five thousand attendees over three days. Where else could you meet a large quantity of high-quality potential customers who are specifically interested in healthcare technology and be able to talk to them directly over such a short period?

Here is a second example. Your CEO may want to partner with companies that have very different products than yours, selling both products to your customers. Combining both products and selling them to customers as one solution will differentiate your business and may help you sell more than you would if you try to sell your product on its own. In this case, you want to exhibit at a show or conference that attracts corporate attendees and exhibitors who are open to signing a business partnership agreement with your organization.

By limiting your goals to a maximum of two, you can target the ideal trade show or conference, which provides the specific audience you need to help you achieve those goals.

Insider insight

Once you have established your goals, you need to ask, "What is the plan for this event? What objectives do I need to put in place to help me achieve the goal?"

(continued)

(continued)

You cannot use the terms *goal* and *objective* interchangeably. They have two very distinct meanings.

Let's define them and review some examples to get you thinking about your organization.

Understanding the difference between goals and objectives

A *goal* is something you want to achieve. For example, your trade show goal might be to:

♦ Generate more qualified leads.

♦ Launch a new product or service to your target audience.

♦ Establish strategic business partnerships with similar companies in your industry.

♦ Cross-sell more services to existing customers.

♦ Gain a deeper understanding of your competitors' products, messaging, positioning, and marketing strategy.

♦ Identify new channel partners who may be interested in re-selling your products and services.

♦ Attract new employees.

While a goal is a wish or desired outcome, it's essential to quantify your goal with specific, numbers-based objectives.

Let's use the goal of generating more qualified leads as an example.

An *objective* is a specific way in which you are going to achieve that goal. For example, if your goal is to generate more qualified leads, how are you going to do that? The answer to that question is your objective.

In this example, your objective may be to speak with at least twenty-five booth visitors per day and label each visitor as a marketing qualified lead (MQL), a sales qualified lead (SQL), or a potential lead that needs long-term nurturing.

Let's take it one step further. Now that you know what you want to achieve at this show and you have an objective of qualifying at least twenty-five booth visitors per day, what tactics are you going to use to make this happen? These are actual actions you and your team will take.

While I am not going to speak about trade show tactics this early in the book, setting specific tactics is the next step on the road to being a successful exhibitor.

A *tactic* is an individual step or action that you can take to help achieve an objective. Since our objective is to qualify twenty-five booth visitors per day, how will we do that?

Your tactics may be:

♦ Write a series of qualifying questions booth staffers can ask of booth visitors.

♦ Educate booth staff on the answers they should expect to receive. These answers will enable them to determine if a visitor is an MQL, SQL, not yet a lead, or will never be a lead.

♦ Enter questions into the lead retrieval device for use by booth staff. The device will enable all answers and contact information to be collected in one central hub and quickly and easily transferred to your internal customer relationship management (CRM) and marketing automation systems.

By evaluating these quantifiable objectives after the show, you can see how close you came to achieving them. It will also help you determine how future event tactics might need to change to achieve your goals.

Chapter 2: Don't Throw Darts with Your Eyes Closed

get your gift

Picking the Right Show

O nce you decide to include trade shows and conferences in your marketing strategy, the question is, "How do you pick the right show?" Follow these steps to determine which trade show will be most appropriate and deliver the best return for your business.

Step 1. Create a list of shows

Create a list of all trade shows that attract your target audience based on your already established goals and objectives.

They may be industry-specific shows, association shows, or shows that focus on a specific need or interest. They may be local shows taking place in your city or town, state-wide or regional shows, national shows, or even international shows.

For example, the Yankee Dental Congress is an annual expo for New England dental professionals.

The London Textile Fair is a fashion industry trade show for businesses interested in fashion and establishing business partnerships.

The American Institute of Certified Public Accountants (AICPA) holds the leading conference and expo for American CPAs.

The BookExpo America (BEA) is a hub for readers, writers, publishers, editors, and everyone else interested in reading, writing, publishing, and marketing books.

Review your list to determine which of the shows would be appropriate for your company's exhibit based on your business goals and your target audience.

Step 2. Include the show's location

Next to each show you just wrote down, include where it is taking place. Is it a local, regional, or national show?

Don't always assume that the largest shows are the best shows. Suppose your business is in Boston, Massachusetts, and you sell custom greeting cards that reference New England landmarks. You will be more successful selling your cards to direct customers and businesses at a smaller regional event that attracts a larger percentage of New England-area attendees than a large national event in New Orleans, Louisiana, that attracts attendees from all over the country but has a significantly smaller number of attendees from New England.

If your sales territory is local or regional and you want to keep it that way, or your product is targeted at a specific geography, spending money on a big national show will not be cost-effective.

Think of it this way. There is a small regional show in Los Angeles that attracts two thousand attendees from the greater Los Angeles and Southern California areas. A similarly focused national show in Chicago, Illinois, attracts 21,000 attendees, but only four hundred of the Chicago show attendees come from Southern California. If your business targets Southern California buyers, you would benefit from the smaller, more targeted, and less expensive show in Los Angeles rather than spending more money on a large national show where fewer of your target customers attend and your business must compete with more exhibitors.

Contrary to popular belief, a larger show is not always better. The show must attract the right attendees.

Step 3. Calculate total event hours

Calculate the total trade show or conference hours. Then break that time down into the amount of time the educational sessions, keynote speeches, or other presentations are taking place, and the amount of time the expo hall is open for attendees to visit exhibitors.

The amount of time allotted for each of these is rarely the same. Some shows allow the expo hall to be open most of the day. Attendees are free to participate in the educational sessions, visit exhibitor booths, set up meetings, and move freely through all areas of the show as they wish. At these shows, the management team has placed equal importance on education and exhibitor visits.

Other shows may be more focused on attendee education rather than expo floor exhibitor sales. In this case, the speaker sessions may run all day, and the expo hall may only be open for a couple of hours over lunch. At these shows, the management team has decided that attendee education is more important than product sales and only allows selling to take place for a limited time.

Here is an example of two shows. Each one has a different focus. Knowing a show's focus and combining it with your understanding of the audience the show attracts will help you make an informed decision about which show will deliver the best return.

TABLE 1. Schedule comparison of two individual trade shows.		
	Show 1	Show 2
Show focus	Speaker sessions and selling on expo floor equally.	Speaker sessions. Minimal selling on expo floor.
Event days	3 days	3 days
Conference hours per day	9:00 a.m.–4:30 p.m.	9:00 a.m.–5:00 p.m.
Expo hall hours	10:00 a.m.–5:00 p.m.	11:00 a.m.–1:00 p.m.
Total show hours	22.5 hours	24 hours
Total expo hall hours	21 hours	6 hours

Note in table 1 that while Show 2 is longer, taking place over twenty-four hours across three days, there are only six hours in which the expo hall will be open for you to meet attendees in your booth vs. twenty-one hours of booth time in the Show 1 example.

Because the expo hall in Show 1 is open fifteen hours longer than Show 2, you may think that exhibiting in Show 1 is a no-brainer. But is your target audience attending? How many are attending? How far will you need to travel for each show?

In Show 2, attendees can only visit the expo hall for six hours. While this is a short amount of time, consider this. If most of the attendees include your target audience and the show is taking place in the town next to your office, you may choose to exhibit.

Why?

Your booth staff will be able to drive to the expo hall. This short distance will eliminate expensive air travel, and hotel rooms will not be needed because they can return to their homes in the evening.

In this example, if the show is taking place in Minneapolis, Minnesota, and your office is fourteen miles away in Mendota Heights, Minnesota, you should add this event to your trade show consideration list for additional research and assessment.

Step 4. Review exhibitor prospectus

Review the exhibitor prospectus or brochure to understand show attendee demographics, how many people attended the show last year, and the number and types of exhibitors.

The show organizer will produce a prospectus or brochure with the sole purpose of enticing people like you to sign an exhibitor contract.

You will most likely find this prospectus in the exhibitor section of the show's website, but if it's not there, reach out to the show's sales department and request a copy.

If the exhibitor prospectus provides information that you believe will generate a positive return for your company, it's time to reach out to the show's sales team to have a more in-depth conversation about the possibility of exhibiting.

Step 5. Ask specific questions of the sales team

Here are some questions you should ask the show's sales team before you make your final decision whether to exhibit or not.

You may come up with others that are important to your specific industry or target audience.

Questions to ask regarding the previous show's results

♦ What was your previous show's total attendee count?

♦ What companies, organizations, vendors, or suppliers exhibited at the last show?

♦ What percentage of the previous show's attendees said they visit the expo hall to find new products and services?

♦ How many attendees said they purchased or directly influenced the purchase of exhibitor products and services?

Questions to ask regarding the upcoming show's sales and marketing strategy

♦ What companies, organizations, vendors, or suppliers have already signed contracts to exhibit at the next show?

♦ What marketing strategies will you use on last year's attendees to get them to register for and attend the next show?

♦ What strategies do you use to market to new show attendees?

♦ Do any other shows take place at the same time in the same convention center? If so, will each show's registered attendees be allowed to visit the other show and their exhibitors?

♦ What is the percentage breakdown of returning attendees vs. new attendees?

♦ What is the percentage breakdown of returning exhibitors vs. new exhibitors?

Questions to ask regarding your exhibitor participation

♦ Are there any strategies exhibitors used in the past that stand out in your mind as being particularly successful in attracting attendees to the exhibitor's booth?

♦ How many exhibitors said the last show exceeded expectations for the number of qualified sales leads received?

♦ What are the attendee demographics? This includes data on men vs. women, businesspeople vs. technical professionals, and attendee buying authority.

Other demographic information that is important to your business

♦ What events, welcome receptions, snack breaks, or other special activities will occur in the expo hall around the exhibitor booths?

♦ Does the expo hall include a café or a large seating/eating area where attendees can rest or work on their mobile devices?

♦ What are some additional benefits included as part of an exhibitor contract? Examples may be, the preregistered attendee list with multiple time use, exhibit staff and attendee badges, free Wi-Fi on the expo floor, complimentary listing in the print and online show guide with contact information and product description included.

Evaluate how each of the answers helps you select the right trade show to meet your company's marketing and business goals.

Free bonus gift available!
Grab your free master list of trade show questions at https://www.lisamasiello.com/trade-show-411-exhibitor-tools.

Chapter 3: Champagne Taste on a Beer Budget

get your gift

Budgetary Considerations

(continued)
budget puts $400,000-$500,000 of their yearly budget toward events.

This budget allocation demonstrates the value they place on exhibiting, speaking at, and sponsoring live in-person events.

W hether you have a $20,000 per year live event budget or a $250,000 per year live event budget to support all the shows you want to attend, an individual trade show budget cannot be created in a vacuum or pulled out of the air.

It takes a combined understanding of your goals and objectives, strategy, and tactics. You must be aware of how much of your yearly marketing budget goes to live events, and how many trade shows, conferences, and other events you will be doing throughout the year.

Selecting a trade show budget that is too high may make you look good at the end of the show because you didn't go over budget. However, those additional funds may cause you to spend money on activities and programs you would not have otherwise considered. You may decide that there is money in the budget, so why not spend it?

Allocating a large budget for one show may also require you to take marketing money away from another show. If you allocated money more accurately, not only could you meet the needs of the first show, but you may also have money to build another product demo kiosk or send another email campaign for the second show.

Selecting a trade show budget that is too low will cause you to go over budget. Variable cost items like drayage may end up taking more of your budget than you expect and cause you to go over budget. Going over budget by $300 or $400 is understandable. Go over budget by $6,000, and your boss will ask what method you will use to ensure this does not happen again.

You may also have been able to close more sales by conducting additional live product demonstrations if you had the money to build another demo kiosk.

Selecting an accurate budget without show goals and objectives will be impossible.

There are multiple elements to take into consideration.

♦ Determine your event budget for the year. What percentage of your total marketing budget is allocated for live events?

♦ Determine how many trade shows and conferences you will attend throughout the year. Create a list of all the events that will be important for your company to exhibit at throughout the year.

♦ What are your goals and objectives for each show?

♦ What is your strategy to achieve your show goals? What tactics will you use?

♦ Determine if each show is local with little travel and hotel accommodations required. Or will travel, hotels, and food be a large portion of your costs?

♦ How many employees will be on your booth staff?

♦ Do you currently have a trade show booth you can reuse with new graphics, or will you need to build a new booth from scratch?

♦ What will the total weight be for all show materials? How far will they have to be shipped?

♦ Will you be able to ship materials to the show's advance warehouse to take advantage of advance warehouse discounts, or will you be sending many of your materials directly to the expo hall?

The show details are where the rubber meets the road

While these questions are essential, they are only the beginning. They are the high-level questions you must answer to help you begin to focus on a more accurate budget.

When added together, hundreds of small details will give you a much more accurate picture of your budget and how you should allocate the money.

The next set of in-depth questions will help you narrow your budget estimate even further. Our goal is to turn the question, "What should our budget be for this show?" from a guesstimate to a more defined estimate. Answer the appropriate questions for your business, eliminate those that don't pertain to you, and add questions and answers unique to your needs.

Booth-specific elements

♦ What size booth space will you reserve? For example, 10 x 10 ft., 10 x 20 ft., 10 x 30 ft., 20 x 20 ft., 20 x 30 ft., 40 x 40 ft., or larger.

♦ What is the booth cost?

♦ Do you have an existing booth structure you can use at this show, or will you need to build a new booth?

♦ Will it be more cost-effective to buy it or rent a booth?

♦ Can you use existing booth graphics, or will you need to design and print new graphics?

♦ What kinds of graphics do you need?

♦ What size and quantity of graphics do you need?

Marketing and sales-related elements

♦ Will you produce and print sales collateral? If so, how many pieces?

- Will you only make your collateral available in PDF format or in print as well?
- What promotional items will you distribute in your booth? How many will you order?
- Will you play any booth games, have a contest, or conduct a drawing?
- What types of prizes will you give away? How many will you give away, and what will their cost be?
- What tool or resource will you use to capture leads? If using a lead retrieval device or tablet, how many will you have?
- Will you pay for a separate show sponsorship in addition to being an exhibitor?

Trade show labor

- What is the cost for the show's union labor or your exhibitor contractor to install and dismantle your booth in the expo hall?
- What is the drayage cost to deliver your booth and booth materials from the expo hall loading dock to your physical booth location before the show begins and back to the loading dock after the show ends?
- What is the cost for other labor-related activities? For example, hanging your company sign from the ceiling.

Shipping

- What is the cost to ship your booth and all additional items, including collateral and graphics, to the advance warehouse before the show begins?
- What is the cost to ship your booth and all additional items, including collateral and graphics, directly to the expo hall loading dock?

Exhibitor services

♦ What is the cost of carpet rental and installation based on the size of the booth space you have selected?

♦ What is the cost of electricity rental and installation based on the booth size and the amount of electricity you need to power your booth?

♦ What is the cost of internet usage in your booth for the duration of the show?

♦ Will you be distributing food in your booth? If so, how much do you expect to hand out? Will you ship the food to your booth, or will you order it from the show-approved caterer? Include the cost of food and any additional fee the show organizer will charge to allow you to distribute food in your booth.

Booth staffing

♦ How many members of your team will staff your booth? Calculate the cost to send yourself and each member of your booth staff from their office to the show city before the show begins and from the show city back to their office after the show is over.

♦ Will hotel rooms be needed? Determine the total number of nights required by each staff member, and calculate the total hotel cost for each of them.

♦ Will transportation be needed for each booth staffer to travel from their hotel to the expo hall each morning and from the expo hall back to the hotel each evening?

♦ How many trade show shirts or other uniform items do you need to order and supply to your staff to wear in the booth? If the show is more than two days, be sure to order more than one shirt per person.

- What clothing sizes will you need to order?
- What will your average daily food cost be per staff member? If your company has a food per diem, use this dollar amount per person, per day.

Marketing campaigns

- Will you place a print ad in the show guide or a trade publication that will have additional distribution at the show?
- Will you do any online advertising promoting your participation at the show?
- Will you do any pre-show and post-show email campaigns?
- Will a member of your company speak at the show? Calculate all expenses related to their presentation including travel, hotel, and food.
- Will you conduct any marketing campaigns or on-site events for current customers?

Additional expenses

- Will your company sponsor an activity, show item, or event such as a keynote speaker, cocktail hour, an educational session track, badge lanyards, afternoon snacks in the expo hall, breakfast, or lunch?
- Will your company rent a hospitality suite for a private meeting or a networking reception? Be sure to include both the cost of the room and refreshments.

While your plans may change over time and prices may increase or decrease slightly, completing this list will give you good insight into what your budget will be for your next show. Then, complete the same process for each show at which you will exhibit this year. Knowing your total trade show budget number and the anticipated budgets for each show enables you to make necessary budget cuts and move money from one show to another.

This event budget and cost breakdown spreadsheet will help you keep track of your expenses and quickly see whether you are under, at, or over budget.

Free bonus gift available!
Grab your free master budgeting spreadsheet at https://www.lisamasiello.com/trade-show-411-exhibitor-tools.

Part 2
Pre-Show Tips

Chapter 4: Brother, Can You Spare a Dime?

Free Money to Exhibit

If I'd only known earlier

In a traditional sales model, a company develops their own products or services, and their sales team sells those products or services directly to businesses or consumers.

In a reseller or channel sales model, a third-party business purchases a manufacturer or vendor's products or services and resells them to other businesses or consumers. While the reseller sales model is most common in the technology industry, you may sell cars, toys, bicycles, medical devices, garden hoses, or drinking glasses. The idea of purchasing products from a vendor or manufacturer and reselling them to other businesses or end-user customers is the same across industries.

Did you know that the vendor from whom you buy your products may have money to help you defray the cost of exhibiting at your next trade show? It could be yours for the asking.

Unless your company is the manufacturer of the products you sell, you most likely resell the products or services of another vendor, supplier, distributor, or manufacturer. The vendor from whom you buy these products expects you to market and sell them.

Why your vendor cares about your trade show

Whether they sell garden hoses or laptop computers, any manufacturer or vendor's objective is to sell as many of their products as possible. They also want you to sell as many as possible.

That's why they make money available to reseller partners like you. They hope that the money they provide you will be used to sell more products successfully.

The money they have available is known as market development funds (MDFs). MDFs are monies the vendor has set aside to offer to select sales partners based on the vendor's specific needs and the potential for their sales partner's success.

If a vendor believes your organization has shown expertise in selling their products or they see your potential for growth and future sales, they may approach you.

These funds are made available at the vendor or manufacturer's discretion to partners like you before any sales occur. The dollar amount can vary from partner to partner.

What you'll need to provide to your vendor to even have them consider giving you money

If you're unsure whether your vendor makes money available to companies like yours, talk to them.

Reach out to their marketing manager or channel partner manager. Tell them you're interested in exhibiting in a specific trade show, and ask if they provide money to their partners to defray the cost of participating.

Be forewarned. Vendors do not just hand out money to every partner who requests it. You will need to provide them with three types of information to help them determine if you should receive the money or not.

1. **Tell the vendor exactly how much money you want.** Don't be wishy-washy. Don't say, "If you could give us between $2,000 and $6,000, that would be great." That's a big spread. Establish your budget ahead of time, and know exactly how much money you want. In a minute, I'll talk about other things you may want to ask for if the vendor cannot provide cash.

2. **Tell the vendor what the event will be like.** Be prepared to answer questions about the show's location, expected attendees, and what you will display in your booth. You may come up with additional questions and answers specific to your industry, your products and services, or areas of interest to your vendor. Here are some questions to get you started:

    *   Where and when will the show take place?
    *   Is this a local, regional, national, or international show?
    *   How many people are currently registered to attend?
    *   How many companies are currently registered to exhibit?
    *   Do you have a list of the companies that have already confirmed they will exhibit?
    *   What is the demographic of the show attendees?
    *   How big will your booth be?
    *   What products or services will be on display in your booth?
    *   Will you be selling only one vendor's products in your booth, or will you be selling products from other vendors as well?

- What is your booth's theme?
- Will you have any special promotions or contests to attract booth visitors?

3. **Tell the vendor what return on investment you expect to achieve.** The vendor wants to feel comfortable that you will spend their money wisely. Be ready to answer questions like:

- To what elements of the show will you allocate the money?
- How many new SQLs do you expect to generate?
- What is your typical conversion rate from SQL to a customer?
- What pre-show and post-show marketing activities will you implement to attract people to your booth, hold on-site meetings, and close post-show deals?

Be prepared for your vendor to ask questions and evaluate the potential return on their investment as closely as you are.

What if your vendor has no MDFs to give you?

If your vendor says there are no funds available, that shouldn't be the end of your conversation.

Continue discussing your plans for the upcoming show. The vendor may encourage you to participate and offer to support you differently. They may:

- Provide products to be demonstrated in your booth.
- Provide a product to be raffled off to your booth visitors.
- Provide tchotchkes to be handed out in your booth.
- Send one or two employees from their office to help.

Although your vendor is not handing you cash, giving you products to demonstrate means you don't have to spend your own money buying them.

Having them send their staff members to help you do booth duty means you can eliminate your employees' travel, hotel, and food expenses because they are no longer going to the show.

If your office is in Atlanta, Georgia, and the show is in Seattle, Washington, the cost savings for you to not send one or two employees from Atlanta to Seattle for four days may be more significant than if your vendor had simply written you a check.

Determine actual ROI and plan for next year

Once the show is over, your vendor will most likely ask you to provide follow-up data on the show's actual results vs. the plan. This information includes how many net new customers you closed or products you sold.

Since you should report this data to your company's management team anyway, the fact that you will also have to provide it to your vendor or manufacturer should not cause a great deal of extra work.

If your show was a success and produced a positive return for both your company and your vendor, they may decide to add this show to their list of marketing activities next year. They may choose to:

♦ Provide you with more money to exhibit again.
♦ Partner with you on a larger booth where you equally share the cost, all marketing resources, and the staff.
♦ Exhibit with their own booth and invite you to display your signage in their booth.
♦ Ask if you would like to join them in a panel discussion.

Receiving MDFs, products to give away, or an additional staff member who works in the booth with your team are some of the best ways to reduce your cost of trade show participation. It can be a win-win opportunity for both you and your vendor, so don't hesitate to discuss this with them.

Chapter 5: One, Two, Three, or More

Booth and Show Passes/Badges

If I'd only known earlier

This chapter will focus on the difference between the full conference pass and the booth or expo-only pass. As an exhibitor, you will receive these passes as part of your booth space purchase.

The most important thing to remember is that you are not limited to the number of passes given to you.

For example, you may be given three exhibit hall passes and one conference pass as part of your 10 x 10 ft. booth price, but you're not limited to only sending four people to the conference. You can choose to send any number of employees that you feel are necessary.

Assign the free exhibitor and conference passes to primary members of your team. Then determine if you will need to purchase additional passes and how many they will be.

A t this point, you know your company's goals for the coming year, you have created a list of trade shows at which your company will exhibit, you have developed a budget for each event, you have reached out to show organizers, and you have signed an exhibitor contract.

As part of the exhibitor package, your company is allocated a specific number of booth and show passes. The number of passes varies based on your booth's size and the show in which you are exhibiting.

A show has two primary types of passes. They each provide a distinct level of access to the events that will occur, and their cost is different.

At a minimum, your show will offer you a full conference pass and a booth or expo-only pass. It may also have a separate pass for the educational sessions or a VIP pass that gives you front-row seating for the keynote presentations or private speaker/author meet-and-greet events.

Let's first define what these passes are and what they include.

Booth or expo-only pass

Give booth or expo-only passes to employees who will work in your booth in the expo hall. For example, my booth staff typically included a couple of people from the sales department, one from marketing, one from product management, one from customer care, and an engineer or other technical professional.

The type of people you choose to include on your team depends on the products and services you sell and your show objectives.

The booth/expo-only pass enables each of your staff members to enter the expo hall during the conference's installation and dismantle hours and one to two hours before the expo doors open on the days when the conference is taking place. This pass only provides access to the expo hall and does not allow access to the show's educational sessions, meetings, keynote speeches, or other events.

Full conference pass

A full conference pass typically includes access to all meetings, educational sessions, keynote speeches, networking events, the exhibit hall, and meals. This is typically the same pass that you would receive if you paid to go to the conference as an attendee.

Each employee who plans to attend all show events and visit the expo hall should have one. You will most likely give this pass to your vice president of sales, your chief executive officer (CEO), or another member of your management team.

How many passes should you expect as part of your exhibitor package?

A 10 x 10 ft. exhibitor booth package generally includes three exhibit-only or booth passes and one full conference pass.

While this is relatively standard, the number of passes you receive will vary from show to show. You may be given more passes or less depending on what that specific show decides is appropriate for their event.

How many more should you buy?

To ensure that you do not buy passes unnecessarily, determine how many staff members you will send to the show. Separate your list into two categories:

Full conference pass

Create a list of those people whose primary focus will be to attend the educational sessions, keynote presentations, and meet with strategic business partners and customers. This list may include your CEO, vice president of sales, CMO, or another senior executive.

Their purpose for attending the show will most likely be to listen to presentations and have strategic meetings with potential business partners or large customers. Please don't add them to your formal booth duty schedule unless they ask you to do so.

Subtract the number of full conference passes you received as part of your exhibitor package from the number of people you included here. That is the number of full conference passes you need to buy.

Insider insight

Your senior management team will stop by your booth when they are free. They may even spend time speaking with booth visitors.

You can let them know that they are very welcome in the booth, and you are happy to have their help and support, but you are not counting on them to staff the booth for a specific length of time.

Since you are your company's exhibitor manager, it is your responsibility to manage everyone's attendance. That includes all employees attending the show to work in the booth or for other reasons. You should register all your company's attendees and provide them with their show passes.

Exhibitor or booth pass

Now create a list of all the people—including yourself—attending the show to work in your booth. These are the people whose primary purpose for attending the conference is to generate qualified leads and close deals.

Your list will include your marketing and sales team members but could also include product managers, engineers, technical support personnel, and customer care representatives. These people should receive the exhibitor passes.

Subtract the number of booth- or exhibit-only passes you received as part of your exhibitor package from the number of people you included here. That is the number of booth passes you will need to buy.

Other show participants from your company

Your marketing director, sales director, or head of customer service may let you know that they are attending the show and are happy to work in the booth on one day of the three-day conference. Still, they want to attend the keynote presentations and participate in networking events to meet with potential business partners.

If this is the case, you will need to determine what access the full conference pass provides them and whether giving them an exhibitor pass is sufficient or if you will need to buy them a full conference pass.

If the keynote presentations and evening networking events are open to all conference participants, no matter what badge they hold, a less-expensive exhibitor pass will be acceptable. If the keynote presentations or other events are open only to those attendees with full conference badges, you will need to pay for full access.

Using the exhibitor package passes can be a substantial cost savings

Here is an example of exhibitor registration cost savings when you use your exhibitor package's passes.

Table 2 includes a sample of items frequently included in a standard exhibitor package. In this example, the package not only includes your rental of the physical booth space but also conference badges or passes, your company's name on the conference website, advertising opportunities, and the ability to use the show's list of preregistered attendees, all for one price.

TABLE 2. Elements of an exhibitor package and associated cost.

Package includes	Cost
10 x 10 ft. inline booth space	$4,500
One full conference badge/pass ($1,795 value)	—
Company listing in the show's mobile app and the conference website	—
Four exhibitor badges/passes per each 10 x 10 ft. space ($400 value)	—
Pre-show advertising opportunities exclusively reserved for exhibitors	—
Access to the preregistered list of attendees to conduct a marketing campaign	—
Total	$4,500

Let's see what happens to the exhibit cost if you use the passes provided in the exhibitor package vs. paying for the same passes separately.

Table 3 includes the cost of the exhibitor package noted in table 2, but the exhibitor did not realize that passes were included.

As a result, they purchased one additional full conference pass and four exhibitor passes above and beyond the money they spent for their exhibitor package.

As you can see by comparing the total cost in tables 2 and 3, you will pay an additional $2,195 if you are unaware that passes are included in your exhibitor package and purchase them separately.

TABLE 3. Total cost to exhibitor if exhibitor passes go unused and passes are purchased separately.

	Cost
Exhibitor package (with unused passes)	$4,500
Full conference pass as additional purchase	$1,795
Four exhibitor passes as additional purchase	$400
Total	$6,695

Insider insight

Follow these steps.

Create your list of those people who will be attending the trade show from your company. Determine their reason for attending. For example, are they attending to sell products in the booth, attending the educational sessions, or having meetings with potential business partners?

1. Assign the free passes you have already received as part of your exhibitor package to the appropriate people. For example, you should give a booth-only pass to a junior salesperson. It would be best if you gave a full conference pass to your CEO.

2. Determine how many additional exhibitor and full conference passes you will need to buy.

Additional insider insight

To avoid the appearance of overcrowding, an exhibitor best practice is to have only two staff members in your booth at any

(continued)

(continued)

given time for every 10 x 10 ft. area. That means if you have a 10 x 20 ft. inline booth, you should have up to four staffers in the booth at the same time. If you have a 30 x 30 ft. island booth, you should have up to eighteen staffers in your booth.

Chapter 6:
Sleep With It Under Your Pillow
Exhibitor Services Manual

If I'd only known earlier

No matter how many trade show exhibits I manage, the exhibitor services manual is my go-to resource.

It is the first thing I review in the morning and the last thing I check at night. I eat with it, sleep with it, and bathe with it. Well, maybe I don't bathe with it, but you get the picture.

Why is it so important that both marketing professionals new to trade show management and exhibitor managers with years of experience get to know the manual's contents from cover to cover? Because every show is different.

City and convention center regulations are different.

Safety requirements are different.

Union rules are different.

What you can and cannot do as an exhibitor is different.

I have managed exhibitor participation at hundreds of trade shows. The exhibitor services manual is still the first piece of information I study as part of my pre-show planning. It should be yours too.

W hether you are new to exhibitor management or have managed hundreds of shows in the past, the exhibitor services manual is your go-to source for information on all aspects of exhibitor participation. It contains everything you need to plan for, prepare for, and execute a successful show, as well as all the rules and regulations you must follow. You will receive your exhibitor services manual after you sign the exhibitor contract. Read it from cover to cover.

The show decorator publishes the exhibitor services manual. Trade show management hires them to install and dismantle the booths, provide general contracting services, lay carpet, hang signs, and decorate the expo hall. The show decorator is also known as a general contractor or the official show contractor. GES and Freeman are two of the most well-known show contractors, but there are many others.

What does the exhibitor services manual include?

The exhibitor services manual includes all the information you as an exhibitor will need to prepare to successfully ship in, install, dismantle, and ship out your booth.

When I started managing exhibits thirty years ago, the exhibitor services manual was a white hard-sided binder given to you once you signed the exhibitor agreement and selected your booth number.

Today, the exhibitor services manual is often a PDF file or multiple PDF files, which you can read online and download as needed. Some shows require you to print out the service forms and fax them to the show decorator. In other cases, the show decorator has an online portal where you can read the exhibitor services manual and reserve your services through their website.

For a small show with five hundred attendees and thirty exhibitor booths located in a hotel ballroom, the exhibitor services manual could be all of twelve pages. A sixty-thousand-attendee show with four hundred exhibitors in the Las Vegas Convention Center may have an exhibitor services manual of 195 pages. No matter the size, you should study it from cover to cover.

Your show's exhibitor services manual may include some of the following items or even more.

♦ Maps of the convention center and floorplans of the expo hall and surrounding meeting rooms
♦ Exhibitor move-in and move-out dates and times
♦ The number of passes provided per 10 x 10 ft. space as well as badge registration and pickup instructions
♦ Essential contact information for show management and additional services, including photography, booth security, lead retrieval, internet services, plant rental, models, and the business center
♦ Exhibitor appointed contractor rules
♦ Security services
♦ Transportation services
♦ International shipping and customs requirements
♦ Insurance requirements
♦ Advance warehouse and on-site freight handling instructions and prices
♦ Hand-carry instructions and limitations
♦ Marshaling yard directions and instructions
♦ Marketing, public relations, and sponsorship opportunities
♦ Housing and hospitality information
♦ Booth rules and regulations including installation and dismantle, height restrictions, signage, construction, noise

levels, cleaning, product demos, electrical, lighting, givea-ways, sampling, pets, vehicles on display, and fire code restrictions

♦ General rules and regulations related to advertising, building damage, photography, smoking, contests, and entertainment

Forms to be completed by you

Your exhibitor services manual will include forms that you must complete and fax or email back to your show decorator.

The show decorator may also have an online portal where you can go to complete the paperwork electronically.

Forms include:

♦ Certificate of liability insurance (all exhibitors must show proof of insurance before they can participate)
♦ Payment authorization form
♦ Exhibitor transportation shipping form (if you are using the show decorator to ship your booth and materials)
♦ Advance warehouse and convention center shipping labels
♦ Electrical services form
♦ Outbound material handling form
♦ Booth cleaning services form
♦ Recycling and trash removal form
♦ Booth installation and dismantle labor form
♦ Telephone and cable TV services form
♦ Plant rental form
♦ Furniture rental form
♦ Catering services form
♦ Lead management/lead retrieval form
♦ Show photography form
♦ Internet services form

If this is your first time exhibiting at a trade show

Read your exhibitor services manual all the way through, from front cover to back cover, in one sitting. It is crucial to get a feel for and understand what requirements you must meet.

Now that you feel entirely overwhelmed, walk away. You need a break from the fire hose of information coming at you.

The next day or two days later, find another time when you have an hour to be able to sit and be quiet. Open your exhibitor services manual and go through it once again. Since you already know what information it includes, you can pay closer attention to the specifics.

There is a lot to digest.

There are thousands of small details.

Things you can do and things you can't do.

Due dates to receive discounts on services.

The deadline after which you can no longer send shipments to the advance warehouse.

Take notes. Create a sorting system using colored Post-it® notes denoting due dates, shipping requirements, services to be ordered, and more.

You need to keep a hard copy of the exhibitor services manual next to you or keep an electronic file open on your computer to quickly refer to it every time you are working on some aspect of your show.

If this is your twenty-first time exhibiting at a show

If you are an experienced exhibitor, you should know what I'm going to say next.

The advice I give to less-experienced marketing professionals applies to you as well. Read the exhibitor services manual from cover to cover.

Every show is different. The convention center is different. The city is different. The labor laws are different. The facility's rules and regulations are different. Your needs will be different.

What is the most important part of the exhibitor services manual?

My short answer to this question is the *advance order deadline*. The advance order deadline is the date by which you must submit your exhibitor services forms to receive advance order discounts. You can save 20–40 percent on show services simply by submitting your forms before the advance deadline has passed. I will talk about this in much more detail in the next chapter.

For you, the most critical part of the exhibitor services manual may be the part you decide to skip over or the one form you forget to submit. With so many individual details, it's essential to read everything and organize well.

Chapter 7: Don't Be the Last Horse Out of the Starting Gate

Advance Pricing Deadline

If I'd only known earlier

I completed all exhibitor services forms and faxed them to the service providers two days before the advance order deadline. I received confirmation from my fax machine that it sent the documents.

I didn't know that while I sent the forms on my end, some vendors did not receive them on the other end.

The appropriate service providers received the booth installation, electrical, and internet forms. The furniture rental, rigging, and lead retrieval service providers did not receive their forms.

Since I never reached out to confirm they received the faxes, I was shocked when I got to the convention center in Las Vegas. I had to complete these three forms again as if they were new requests.

Not only did I have to pay the higher on-site fee for each service, but they also had me wait hours in queue for the services to be implemented.

(continued)

(continued)
Moral of the story? Confirm all your forms are received ahead of the advance pricing deadline.

L et's stay on the topic of the exhibitor services manual for this chapter as well.

The show decorator and other service providers want you to send your completed forms early, so they offer a discount to exhibitors who submit their order forms approximately one month before the show occurs. The actual amount of time varies from show to show. As you review the due dates for form submission, create an Excel spreadsheet, which you can tack up in front of you and refer to often. Alternatively, you can attach a Post-it note or colorful sticky flag to each of the forms you will complete and submit.

The discount can range between 20 and 40 percent if you pay before the advance deadline rather than waiting until a week or two before the show takes place. Then you will pay the on-site show price.

Meeting the advance deadline is one of the best ways for you to save a lot of money.

Example of exhibitor cost savings
Trade show date: September 28–30

In this example, a trade show is taking place September 28–30. Exhibitors can receive a discount of up to 40 percent if they order services by September 5. Note that this date is twenty-three days before the show begins.

Let's use these dates to determine how much money you, as an exhibitor, can save by ordering services before the advance order deadline of September 5.

TABLE 4. Price comparison of services ordered before and after advance order deadline

	Price Before Deadline	Price After Deadline	Percent Savings (%)
Booth installation labor Four laborers for eight hours straight time to set up a 20 x 30 ft. booth. No overtime rate.	$2,827.20	$3,675.20	23
Booth dismantle labor Requirements to install and dismantle the booth are the same.	$2,827.20	$3,675.20	23
Vacuum booth carpet 20 x 30 ft. booth for three days.	$750.00	$990.00	24
Electrical services 110/120 Volt, 1,000 Watts (10 amps)	$156.00	$234.00	33
Carpet rental and installation 20 x 30 ft. classic carpet with single-layer padding and plastic (Visqueen) covering.	$1,604.10	$2,085.30	30
Furniture rental Round meeting table with four chairs.	$1,058.00	$1,325.45	20
Rigging to hang exhibitor sign One forklift with the operator lifting up to 5,000 lb. and two riggers in a forklift cage to hang a sign. Two hours to hang. No overtime rate.	$799.00	$1,038.80	23

TABLE 4 *(continued)*
Price comparison of services ordered before and after advance order deadline

	Price Before Deadline	Price After Deadline	Percent Savings (%)
Rigging to remove exhibitor sign Requirements to install and remove the sign are the same.	$799.00	$1,038.80	23
Car detailing Car displayed in the booth. Professional detailing before the show begins and daily maintenance for four days.	$375.00	$425.00	12
Audiovisual equipment Two 46-in. flat-screen monitors to run exhibitor videos.	$1,200.00	$1,560.00	23
Drayage Twelve thousand pounds of crated material shipped to the advance warehouse before the September 5 deadline vs. the same 12,000 lb. shipped to the show site on September 26 and is not within the target delivery time.	$9,900.00	$12,180.00	19
Lead retrieval Rental of three tablets with custom questions enabled, wireless printer, delivery, setup, and staff training.	$2,250.00	$2,505.00	10
Total cost:	$24,545.50	$30,732.75	
Total savings:	$6,187.25		

As you can see, by submitting your forms before the discount or early bird deadline, you save $6,187.25. That is a total savings of 20 percent. That's a large amount of money you can use for another lead generation program or other marketing activity.

Insider insight

As you read through your exhibitor services manual, the services that offer advance payment discounts will be obvious. But there are also less-apparent opportunities to save money. Put another way, there are other ways to spend money unnecessarily and exceed your budget. For example:

♦ You do not reserve your sleeping rooms in the show hotel until after the hotel's room block deadline has passed. Rooms may still be available, but you will have to pay full price.

♦ You must pay rush charges to print collateral, graphics, and promotional items shortly before the show is to begin.

♦ You must pay overnight shipping charges to ensure the collateral, graphics, and promotional items get to your booth before the show begins.

Additional insider insight

When referring to the exhibitor services manual, there are two critical tips to remember. We've already addressed them, but they are important enough to mention again.

The requirements for every trade show are different.

The building structure is different.

(continued)

(continued)

The labor laws are different.

The fire regulations are different.

You must read the exhibitor services manual for each show from beginning to end—no matter how experienced you may be at trade show management.

Have the date of each show's exhibitor services form advance deadline burned into your memory and submit your completed forms before that deadline. Trade shows can be extremely costly, so any money you can save will benefit your company and your budget. By waiting until the deadline has passed and then submitting your forms, you are throwing money away. It's as simple as that.

Chapter 8: Mining for Gold

Preregistered Attendee List

Lead generation doesn't just happen in your booth at the show. It begins well before the show takes place. Pre-show marketing and lead generation activities are an effective way for attendees to get to know your company, the products you sell, and special promotions or discounts you will offer during the show.

Consider this. Whether a trade show is a small daylong event with twenty-five exhibitors and five hundred attendees or a large international event with 350 exhibitors and 75,000 attendees, each attendee is going to the event with a specific goal in mind.

Attendees take one, two, three, or more days out of their busy schedules, and they need to justify that what they are going to see and learn will benefit them in a specific way. Trade shows and conferences have multiple educational sessions taking place at the same time. Attendees can't possibly see all of them.

Visiting exhibitor booths may also be an important element of the attendee's priority list. Still, business, industry, and customer meetings may cut into the time they planned on spending in the expo hall.

Trade show attendees begin to seriously evaluate a trade show's business opportunities one and a half to two months before it occurs. They review the educational sessions and begin to develop a list of speakers and topics that they decide are not to be missed.

They reach out to industry colleagues, suppliers and vendors, customers, possible business partners, and other contacts to schedule meetings during the day and dinners in the evening.

They review the exhibitor list to determine which booths they must visit.

Not to be forgotten, the networking parties and the everyday work of responding to emails from people back at the office need to be factored into their schedule as well.

Your job as an exhibitor is to grab their attention and ensure they are interested enough in your company that they begin to build a relationship with your team, stop by your booth, and have an in-depth conversation. If you wait to reach out to attendees and try to attract their attention at the show, their schedule is already full. While they may pass by your booth and stop for a five-minute chat, you have lost the opportunity to introduce your company to them before the show occurs and turn them into a customer in your booth.

It is easier to close the deal in your booth when you've already laid the groundwork rather than trying to lay the sales groundwork in the booth and attempting to close it after the show. Post-show, the lead has returned to their office, and they are focused on other tasks at hand. The show is now out of sight and out of mind. It will be more challenging to get them to refocus on what you're selling.

The preregistered attendee list

Depending on the type of show you have chosen, the exhibitor package you selected, or booth size you decide to purchase, you may be given the preregistered attendee list by the show management team. Usually provided as an Excel spreadsheet, this precious list contains the names, email addresses, and other contact information of the people who have already registered for the show.

You already know that the contacts on this list see enough value in the trade show they have committed to attending. You don't need to convince them that this is the right show for them. Use this opportunity to introduce them to your company. Tell them what you will be presenting at the show. Entice them to stop by your booth by offering a special deal or promotion. Encourage them to set up an in-person meeting with a member of your sales team.

Market to these people both before and after the show. Before the show, create an email drip campaign informing them of your participation or send a direct mail piece with a particular call to action. Invite them to stop by your booth. Tell them that if they mention a unique offer code or present the actual direct mail piece at your booth, they will receive a gift. You will attract additional attendees to your booth and better understand your campaign's success by the number of people who stop by.

You can include other information such as:

♦ What you will promote at the show.
♦ If you will be speaking. The time, date, and location of your speaker session. The name and title of the person from your company who will be speaking. Their topic of discussion.
♦ Key competitive differentiators.
♦ A unique sales offer that will only be available for the length of the show.
♦ Your booth number (including a visual cue such as near the entrance, attendee lounge, or another quickly spotted location).
♦ If you have a hospitality suite for meetings or a networking reception, they should register to attend.

This preregistered list of show attendees should also be made available to your sales team. Encourage them to call every person on the list both before and after the show.

Of course, trolling your in-house sales and marketing database, creating an event web page, telling your social media community, including the information in your prospect and customer newsletters, and adding it to your employees' email signatures are all ways to inform a much wider audience of your participation.

You can do this through drip campaigns, online promotion, email signatures, and your social media community connections.

For this chapter's purpose, however, my focus is on the value of the often-overlooked preregistered attendee list.

Chapter 9:
Everyone Needs to
Row in the Same Direction

get your gift

Exhibitor Staffing

If I'd only known earlier

I once asked my most junior marketing staff member to work with me in our company's booth at a trade show in London. He had never worked at a trade show and never traveled outside of the United States. He was so excited about the upcoming trip.

I provided him with our week-long booth schedule and after-hours agenda. Noticing that there were networking events, parties, and customer dinners each evening, he asked if I was okay with him drinking alcohol at those events.

I answered him with this:

> *You are the face of our company at this show. You are representing our brand both in and out of the booth. How you act reflects on you and the company. You are also a grown man and what you choose to drink is up to you. Drink whatever you want and as much as you want. But remember, you better be in our booth on time the next morning, ready to greet our visitors with a welcome and a smile. That's what you're there for.*

W hile trade show booth staffing is just one element of successful exhibiting, it can be a make-or-break element.

You may have the best products on the market.

You may have gone all out on your pre-show marketing activities.

Still, if attendees get to your booth and staff are on their cell phones or are sitting in the corner with their shoes off, your potential customers will walk by without ever stepping foot in your booth.

They'll never have an opportunity to learn how great your products are because your staff is doing everything but engaging with them.

In chapter 2, I talked about how to evaluate a trade show before you sign the contract. A thorough evaluation helps ensure you pick the show that attracts your target audience. Now it's time to select your booth staff.

Go back and open the exhibitor prospectus you originally received when you were considering exhibiting at the show. The prospectus includes the demographic information on the previous year's attendees such as the type and size of businesses represented, the titles and positions of most attendees, and more.

Let's use the example of a water management trade show. Based on the attendee survey conducted by the show's management team, participants areas of interest generally fall into four categories:

- ◆ Evaluate new water treatment options.
- ◆ Listen to the perspectives of other experienced professionals in the industry.
- ◆ Learn how to better evaluate water management and waste treatment technologies.
- ◆ Provide enhanced customer service to their communities.

TABLE 5. Primary reasons for attending the show

	Percent of attendees (%)
Evaluate water treatment options.	66
Hear from industry professionals.	42
Discover new technologies.	18
Uncover enhanced customer service options.	9

TABLE 6. Attendee title/position

	Percent of attendees (%)
Vice president/COO/manager/director	50
Project manager	20
Marketing representative	15
Field service professional	7
Water conservation specialist	5
Industry analyst	3

A prospectus from a large national or international show may also include the attendee country-of-origin. It may look something like table 7.

What elements of the attendee information stand out to you as crucial demographic information?

What information could help you put together the perfect group of employees to be your booth staff?

TABLE 7. Attendee country of origin	
	Percent of attendees (%)
United States	30
Canada (eastern)	25
Mexico	20
Germany	5
China	5
India	5
Other	10

In table 7, 45 percent of non-US attendees are from Mexico and eastern Canada. Considering that English is not the native language of Mexican attendees, you may want to ask if any of your potential booth staff also speak Spanish. Similarly, residents of eastern Canada may be more comfortable speaking French than English. You might want to consider adding a French-speaking employee to your booth staff.

There are two critical components to exhibitor staffing. They are the number of people you need based on the size of your booth and the type of people you need based on your company's goals.

How many people do you need on your booth staff?

Selecting your trade show booth staff may seem like just another one of those tactical items to check off your to-do list. It's actually much more involved and strategic than that. It is a critical question.

First, you do not want booth visitors to be so overwhelmed with graphics, furniture, displays, demos, literature stands, and booth staff that they choose to walk by rather than engaging with your team.

Second, selecting the wrong people to be part of your booth staff can be disastrous and eliminate any chance of having a positive return on your investment.

An example of the *wrong people* may be a sales professional who is an expert at selling your product or service to doctors in the medical industry but has no experience selling to attorneys in the legal sector who may be the largest group of show attendees. Also, a member of your booth staff who is not used to attending trade shows and is not comfortable speaking with the public may not be the best representative of your company and your products.

To be sure you select the right people for your booth, answer these questions when preparing for a show. Because your goals and objectives will be different for each show, you may select other people based on various criteria.

What are your one or two primary goals for this show?

Before you can select the right people to staff your booth, you must determine your goal for the show. If your goal is to generate many high-quality leads for your sales team back home, your booth staff should include people who have years of experience selling to your customers.

If you are launching a new technical product to chief information officers and information technology (IT) directors, you want to make sure that your staff includes managers and engineers who developed the product and can answer in-depth technical questions.

As you can see, establishing your goal comes first. Then, you select the people who have the experience and expertise to help you achieve that goal.

What roles will be most effective in answering attendee questions and positioning your company based on the goal you have selected?

While your booth staff should consist of various people, including those from marketing, sales, product management, engineering, and customer care, travel expenses and booth size may limit you to a smaller group than you want to send.

As I already mentioned, think about what expertise or knowledge is needed.

List the actual names of team members you would like to work in your booth

This is self-explanatory.

Is each person you are considering confident and knowledgeable enough to speak with the public about your company and products?

Put another way, do they have the *soft skills* needed to interact with many different types of people? Consider knowledge or experience and soft skills separately for each person.

You may have a very experienced sales manager, but he likes to gossip about your company. While this person certainly can speak intelligently about your products, you don't want them to discuss their negative feelings about the company with potential customers.

You may want to consider sending a slightly less-experienced member of the sales team who has a positive attitude and enjoys meeting new people.

Putting product knowledge aside, would you be happy to have each of your proposed booth staffers be the face of your organization and represent your business to potential customers?

Are the people you selected to staff the booth available to participate during the show dates?

Once you put together your booth staff wish list, reach out to each of these people. Discuss the show, the audience, your goals, and why you feel they would be a perfect member of your trade show team.

You want to make them excited about the opportunity and their participation.

You also want to see if they are available. They may be on vacation during the show. They may have a business trip planned at the same time or are unable to attend because they need to stay home with their children.

If someone is unable to attend, think about other employees with similar skills and expertise who might participate in their place.

Not all your company's attendees will be part of your booth staff

Don't schedule your CEO or other senior executives to do booth duty. While they will attend the trade show, their objective may be to conduct strategic business, meet with target customers, and attend the keynote presentations.

Let them know that you certainly welcome their booth participation, but you won't include them in your formal booth duty schedule.

Most company executives like to spend some time in the booth chatting with potential customers as time permits, but that is not their primary objective for attending the conference.

Know the size of your booth

Before you create your booth duty spreadsheet, consider how many staff members should be in your booth at any given time.

The trade show industry's best practice is to allocate one booth staffer for every 50 sq. ft. of available booth space. What I mean by "available booth space" is empty space, meaning space that is free of your booth structure, literature stands, demo stations, or other structural elements.

Let's use a 10 x 20 ft. inline booth as an example.

A 10 x 20 ft. booth is 200 sq. ft. Using the trade show industry best practice of 50 sq. ft. per staff member means a total of four staff members could conceivably be in your booth at any given time.

The reality is that you may want to have two or three staff members in the booth at any given time. Your booth structure, furniture, and other elements will limit the area each person has to stand and limit the number of attendees who can comfortably enter the booth to speak with your staff.

Know the amount of time the expo hall is open per day

In this example, let's say the expo hall will be open from 10:00 a.m. to 6:00 p.m. for three days.

The maximum amount of time that anyone should be required to do booth duty is four consecutive hours. You may want to reduce that time to three hours or even two hours, depending on the number of people you have on your booth staff.

Multiplying our total hours by three days, we will need to staff the 10 x 20 ft. booth for a total of twenty-four hours. We will have three staff members in the booth for four-hour intervals, and each staff member needs to staff the booth for two rounds of four hours each.

Eight hours of booth duty per day require three staff members for four hours each in the morning and an additional three staff members for four hours each afternoon.

Three days of availability with two rounds of booth duty per person means you will need nine people to staff your booth for a total of twenty-four hours over three days.

Answer the following questions about your potential team

- How many members of your team can you afford to send to the show?
- How many people can you afford to have out of the office for the length of the show?
- What level of expertise does each member of the team have?
- Will each person be available for the entire length of the show?
- Will someone have to arrive after the show has already begun or leave the show before it is over?

If the show occurs in your office's city, it is easy for each staffer to leave your office and arrive at the convention center for their scheduled booth duty and return to your office after it is over. They will not be out of the office for the entire length of the show, and you will not incur any hotel expenses.

If your office is in New York City and the show occurs in San Francisco, California, you may not have the budget to fly nine booth staffers plus yourself to San Francisco for a minimum of three days. The airfare, hotel stay, local transportation, and food expenses for each person will add up quickly.

You want a well-staffed booth with team members who have diverse expertise and can answer many different types of questions.

That includes technical and non-technical questions. You also want them to have experience in a specific industry or market and understand your product inside and out.

Use the information we have just reviewed to put together an ideal list of booth staff members. Then review each person and your budget to determine if you will have to tweak anything to create your final list.

Train your booth staff

Even experienced salespeople and executives need training.

They need to understand who the audience will be and what the attendees expect to get out of the show. They need to know the key messages you want them to get across when speaking with prospects in the booth.

- ♦ Is there anything you want them to look for or help you with—putting the booth together or getting competitive intelligence?
- ♦ How is the booth going to look? How will it be laid out? Will you have demo stations or a place to have a private customer meeting?
- ♦ Where will the excess literature and giveaways be stored to enable booth staff to quickly and easily refill literature stands and promotional items?

Have a video conference—or at least a conference call—two to three weeks before the show. The call ensures everyone has their show registration, knows where to go, what hotel they are staying in, and what the company uniform is. Have another call three days before the first person leaves for the show to remind them to pack things like show shirts and business cards.

The philosophy of exhibiting is not every person for themselves. Exhibiting is a team sport. Your booth visitors can sense whether you are all working together as a team, effortlessly handing off conversations from one expert to another, or uncertain about who has what responsibility.

A ten-minute all-hands meeting in the booth the morning of opening day is not enough to make your booth staff gel as one. If you work for a large company or have offices in different cities, some of your team members may have never met one another until they all arrive at the show.

Schedule a dinner at a local restaurant the night before the show begins and bring your booth staff together in a friendly and unhurried environment. This casual get-together will enable them to get to know everyone on a personal level.

About an hour before the expo hall opens on the first day, require that all staff meet in your booth for an in-booth meeting. While you should have already explained to your team all the things that will go on in the booth (for example, games you will play, product demos to be conducted, video or live presentations, and more), it's vital for your team to get the lay of the land in the booth before the show begins.

Walk them around the booth and show them where the demo stations are. Tell each person where you expect them to stand or what responsibilities they will have. Tell them where the extra product literature, pens, and giveaway items are, so they know how to replace the supply when it runs out. Have them test the lead retrieval devices on each other to understand how to use them as visitors enter the booth.

This additional time on-site will reacquaint them with all the information you already provided and enable you to explain what you expect of each of them within the booth surrounding.

Free bonus gift available!

Grab your free master staffing spreadsheet at
https://www.lisamasiello.com/trade-show-411-exhibitor-tools.

Chapter 10: Don't Play Pin the Tail on the Donkey

insider insight

Perfect Booth Size and Location

(continued)
We were able to use that booth location to our advantage. We introduced the Microsoft team to our company and began to build a long-lasting business relationship.

A rguably, the two most frequently asked questions I get from first-time exhibitor managers are what booth size should I select to generate the most ROI for the least cost and where should I locate my booth in the hall?

There is no standard answer to either question. It depends on the goals, needs, and limitations of each exhibiting company.

Let me try to answer these questions in a way that gets you thinking about your own company's needs.

Q: What size booth do I need?
A: As I mentioned, it depends on your goals, needs, and limitations.

My questions to you are:

Why have you decided to exhibit at this show and what are your goals and objectives?

Let's suppose you will use a trade show to launch a new business application that enables users to quickly access large databases of information from any location with 100 percent on-demand availability and easy integration with Microsoft Office and Google Workspace applications.

You may want to have two, three, or four demo stations where you can demonstrate the speed and quality of service to trade show attendees and encourage them to sign up on the spot for a thirty-day free trial.

You will need room in the booth to locate the demo kiosks or tables, additional floor space for two or three people to stand around each demo station, and all other materials you will include in the booth. Using this example, you will not be able to fit all these things into a 10 x 10 ft. inline booth. You should consider a 20 x 20 ft. island or peninsula booth.

If, on the other hand, your goal is not to generate leads but to meet with representatives from Microsoft, Amazon, and Google to discuss possible business partnerships, a 10 x 10 ft. inline booth may be big enough to have small standup conversations with representatives from each of these companies.

What will you do in the booth?

Will you have private meetings, give a presentation, play games, hold a reception, present new products, or conduct product demonstrations? Each of these activities and the number of materials you decide to bring into the space will require a different size booth. Don't forget that your staff and trade show visitors will also take up booth space.

What is your budget?

Not only will you have to pay for your booth structure and all materials in it, but you will first have to pay for the booth space itself. That is the cost you pay to the show organizer or management team to allow you to exhibit at the show. It gets you an area of concrete on the floor of the convention center's expo hall. You are renting a taped-off area 10 x 10 ft., 10 x 20 ft., 30 x 30 ft., or another size on the floor, which could cost you $4,000, $5,500, or more dollars to just rent the space.

This space is the first in a long line of expenses you must pay, including the booth structure, product literature, graphics, giveaway items, and so much more. Calculate your entire show budget and then begin to break down how much of that money you will allocate to the space, booth, and other materials.

If your total budget is $10,000 and your show is on the other side of the country, you will be limited to a 10 x 10 ft. booth because shipping costs will eat up a significant percentage of that budget. If the show is in the same city as your office, the transportation and shipping cost will be small. You may be able to use the money normally allocated for shipping to expand to a 10 x 20 ft. booth space.

The short answer to this question is that the amount of money in your overall budget that you can commit to the booth space will go a long way in determining the maximum size you can afford.

Q: Which booth location is best?
A: Like your question about your booth's size, this depends on your goals and objectives.
My questions to you are:

Will a competitor of yours also have a booth at the show?
If so, do you want your booth to be near them or far away from them? Some companies like direct competition and select a location next to their competitor to go head-to-head. Others prefer to rent a booth on the other side of the hall so there can be no direct comparison by show attendees of the two companies and their products.

Are you interested in establishing a business relationship or partnership with any other exhibiting company?
If so, it will benefit you to reserve a booth as close as possible to the other company's location. The proximity enables your team and the other company's team to evaluate each other, watch what's

going on in each booth, and engage in business conversations during times of low booth traffic.

Are there areas in the expo hall where attendees tend to congregate in large numbers?

For example, in the first row of booths by the expo hall entrance. Near the food concessions. Close to where show management will place the bars during the evening expo hall receptions. Next to the expo hall's seating area where attendees can sit at round tables to work, meet with colleagues, or rest their feet.

Which booth spaces are still available, and which have the most sides open to aisles?

If this is your first time exhibiting at a specific show, you will need to wait to make your space selection until many of the booths are already reserved.

No matter what area of the hall you select, make sure that as many sides of your booth are open to aisles as possible. Aisle access enables attendees to see and easily enter your booth from multiple directions.

Of course, a large 30 x 30 ft. island booth has all four sides open to attendee traffic, but you may not have the budget or need the space for that size booth.

If all you need is a 10 x 10 ft. or even a 10 x 20 ft. booth, highlight the location of available end-cap booths or peninsula booths in your floor plan. A corner booth in a slightly less busy section of the hall is still a better location than the booth tucked in the middle of a long linear row in a somewhat more desirable location.

The standard booth types from which you can choose are:

♦   Linear or inline booth

- Perimeter wall booth
- End-cap booth
- Peninsula booth
- Split island booth
- Island booth

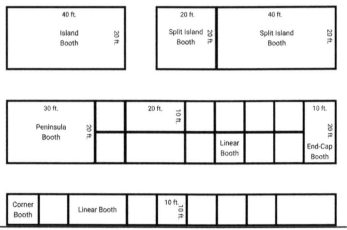

Linear (inline) booth

A linear booth is standard and the most common booth among trade shows of all sizes. It is also known as an inline booth. Only one of its four sides is open to an aisle, and it shares its other two sides and back wall with other exhibitors. Linear booths are arranged next to each other in a straight line.

- **Size options:** The standard size of a linear booth is 10 x 10 ft., but you can purchase two 10 x 10 ft. booths, turning it into one 10 x 20 ft. booth. This larger booth provides 20 ft. of frontage along the aisle where attendees walk.
- **Benefit:** A 10 x 10 ft. linear booth is the least expensive booth space.

♦ **Drawback:** A standard 10 x 10 ft. linear booth is in an aisle with another booth on either side. If you can spend a bit more money, a 10 x 10 ft. corner booth is a great alternative. It is located at the end of a row of linear booths, with two sides open to intersecting aisles. You cannot hang signs from the ceiling over a linear booth. The maximum height of your booth structure is limited to 8 ft.

Insider insight

Each booth type has a different height restriction to ensure attendees walking by can see exhibitors from the aisles.

Whether you rent or buy a booth structure, be sure to provide your height limitation to the exhibit house or contractor supplying your booth.

It is much easier to build the structure to the height limitation from the beginning than to reduce your booth's height after it is in place in your location at the show.

Perimeter wall booth

A perimeter wall booth is a standard linear booth that only has one of its four sides open to an aisle and shares its two sides with other exhibitors.

The difference between a linear booth and a perimeter booth is that the perimeter booth's back wall is set against the expo hall's wall. There is no other exhibitor behind the booth.

♦ **Size Options:** The standard size of a linear booth is 10 x 10 ft., but you can purchase two 10 x 10 ft. booths, turning them into one 10 x 20 ft. booth. This larger booth provides 20 ft. of frontage along the aisle where attendees walk.

◆ **Benefit:** Maximum height is 12 ft. Notice that this is different from a standard linear booth whose maximum height is
8 ft. The reason is that a linear booth shares its back wall
with another exhibitor directly behind it.

◆ **Drawback:** Just like a standard 10 x 10 ft. linear booth, you
have another exhibitor's booth on either side of you unless
you choose a corner booth that also happens to be against
the perimeter wall of the expo hall. You cannot hang signs
from the ceiling over a perimeter wall booth.

End-cap booth

An end-cap booth sits at the end of two rows of linear booths.

◆ **Benefit:** A 10 x 20 ft. end-cap booth enables you to open
three sides of your booth to intersecting aisles. These aisles
increase foot traffic in front of your booth from attendees
walking in different directions.

◆ **Drawback:** Although an end-cap booth does provide you
with more exposure to attendees than a standard linear
booth, it also comes with a higher cost.

If you are interested in purchasing an end-cap booth space, be
sure to speak with the show decorator on their height requirements
for that location so you don't obstruct visitors' views to the booths
behind you.

Peninsula booth

A peninsula booth is like an end-cap booth in that it sits at the end
of two rows of linear booths.

The difference is that a peninsula booth is larger in size at 20 x
20 ft. or more.

A peninsula booth may also share a wall with another peninsula booth. This configuration is known as a split island booth.

- **Benefit:** Just like an end-cap booth, a peninsula booth provides considerably more foot traffic because your booth is open to three main aisles. A hanging sign is allowed over a peninsula booth.
- **Drawback:** If you are seriously considering a peninsula booth and the cost is not a concern, why not step up to an island booth, which can provide the best of all worlds? With an island booth, you are allowed maximum height throughout your space, all four sides are open to an aisle, and attendees can see it from a greater distance.

Island booth

An island booth is 20 x 20 ft. or larger and open to intersecting aisles on all four sides.

- **Benefit:** In an island configuration, your booth will stand alone, enabling you to invite attendees into your space from all four sides. You can also hang signage from the ceiling and have fewer height restrictions within your booth.
- **Drawback:** Other than the higher cost, there are few, if any, drawbacks to an island booth.

Insider insight

If all island booths are reserved before you select your space, evaluate the floor plan to determine if you can create an island booth by purchasing four contiguous linear booths.

(continued)

(continued)

Depending on the show's popularity and the number of exhibitors yet to select their space, show management may or may not reconfigure the area to meet your needs. It never hurts to ask.

Chapter 11:
To Own or Not to Own, That Is the Question

Rent or Own Your Booth

If I'd only known earlier

Your physical booth structure is one of the most expensive components of your exhibitor budget. But cost alone should not be the only factor in deciding if you should rent a booth or have a custom booth built for your company.

By the time the decision to rent or buy your booth comes up, you have most likely already selected the show or shows you will attend and established your budget. While show selection and budget will impact your decision to rent or to own, there are other important factors to consider.

Step back and consider the rent vs. buy question from the 37,000 ft. level. It's a strategic question that will impact much more than simply the next show. There are benefits to each option.

There are advantages to buying your own booth. If you exhibit at three or more shows per year, incurring the expense upfront to buy a booth and then using the same booth for multiple shows will pay for itself over time. Just remember, there will be an ongoing expense to update graphics and fix or replace parts.

Using the same booth with the same look and feel over multiple shows will enable you to maintain consistent corporate branding.

The booth can be customized to your company's exact needs and look and feel. You determine the materials used, the types and number of graphics, the lighting, and the flooring. Do you want a central tower with a spinning sign that extends out to the four corners of the booth and connects to free-standing product kiosks? You can do it.

There are also advantages to renting a booth. Renting a booth is a good option for a company new to trade show exhibiting that wants to put its toe in the water to see what sort of return it will realize. The adage *try before you buy* applies here.

Booth rental is also a good option for companies that will be rebranding or repositioning themselves soon. You don't want to buy a custom booth and have to build an entirely new booth six months later after a rebranding or an acquisition occurs.

When you rent a booth, there are no additional expenses for booth storage and maintenance. Storage and maintenance will be ongoing expenses if you buy a booth.

To help determine if you should rent or buy your trade show booth, answer the following questions.

How much of your trade show budget is for booth building and graphics?

Chapter 3 discusses breaking your budget into specific categories like building the booth, shipping, exhibitor services, staffing, travel, and marketing campaigns.

Once the show is over, this separation will enable you to better evaluate whether you achieved your return on investment.

The Center for Exhibition Industry Research, also known as CEIR, reports that, on average, exhibitors spend 11 percent of their trade show budget on booth design and development, including graphics.

How much money you choose to spend should be based on your company's goals, how many shows you decide to exhibit at over a year, if exhibiting at live events is a priority for you, if you can cut a large check upfront, and if you can manage the ongoing costs for booth storage and rehab. If you choose to buy your booth, you must also factor in your booth structure's insurance cost. If you rent a booth, the exhibit house will be responsible for the insurance.

Will you exhibit at more than one show at the same time or within a limited time frame?

Over the years, it was not uncommon for me to be responsible for the movement of our custom-built booth from a show in Washington, DC, to Orlando, Florida, to Houston, Texas, and to San Francisco, California, all in one month.

Multiple stops over a limited time frame required me to send the original booth and graphics to Washington and then split them up at the end of that show. I shipped specific components of the booth structure and graphics to Orlando and the rest of the booth and graphics to Houston for two smaller shows taking place simultaneously.

Then, when both the Orlando and Houston shows were over, each shipment was sent separately to San Francisco, where the contents were put together again as one large booth.

Making sure you put the right booth pieces in the right boxes, shipping them off in different directions, ensuring everything arrives at the expo hall and is installed on time requires attention to detail and a lot of coordination. It also requires more money. The rush charges you pay to ship a 10 x 20 ft. booth from Orlando to San Francisco in three days may be almost as much as you could pay to rent a booth in San Francisco. And, when you rent a booth, you eliminate the roundtrip shipping expenses.

When booths are shipped directly from one show to the next, there is no time for the exhibit house to assess whether any signs or displays are damaged and require replacement.

Once the booth gets to its destination, is installed, and you take a good look at the structure, you may incur additional rush or over-time expenses to have the show decorator or a local exhibit house fix or clean something that was broken, damaged, or soiled at the previous show.

Renting vs. buying a booth doesn't have to be an either/or de-cision. For example, you may decide to buy a custom booth that you will use at the big national shows three times per year. Then, you will rent a booth for each of the smaller regional or local shows you attend at other times of the year.

Will your booth footprint vary from show to show?

That is, you will exhibit at the first show in a 10 x 10 ft. booth space, and you will have a large 30 x 30 ft. island booth space at the fol-lowing show.

Review your list of trade shows and note the size of each booth space. If you are exhibiting at five trade shows in the next year, will the booth space be a 10 x 10 ft. inline, a 10 x 20 ft. peninsula, or a 20 x 20 ft. island? Will the size be the same for every show, or will each show be different?

If the size is the same, you could easily use the same booth struc-ture at every show.

If the size is different at every show, you must consider this when speaking with your exhibit house and design the booth structure and graphics in a more modular style.

Individual pieces such as demonstration kiosks or product displays can easily be added or removed depending on each booth space's size.

You can certainly build a purchased booth in this way, but this is a discussion you must have with your exhibit house at the first meeting.

If your company has never exhibited before and you are using an upcoming show to determine whether a trade show is a good marketing tactic for your business, you may want to rent a booth, evaluate your participation, and assess your post-show return on investment. Then you can make the final decision as to whether you will rent or buy moving forward.

Will the same signage and messaging be used from show to show, or will they change based on each show's unique audience?

If your graphics are oddly shaped or custom-sized, you may want to buy your booth. Rental booths usually include industry-standard components so that many different exhibitors can use the same sized graphics, lighting displays, and other parts.

If you do not require custom cuts or mounted signs but simply want to change your message for each show audience, a rented booth will enable you to do just that.

Renting the same booth for two shows and replacing the first show's healthcare message with new graphics for the second show's restaurant owner audience will enable you to purchase two signs with unique messages rather than paying for and storing a whole new booth.

Do you have an area to store the booth structure or is there money in your budget to have your exhibit house store your booth between shows?

A rented booth will go back to the company from whom you rented it after the show, and you never have to think about it again.

A purchased booth will need to be stored when not in use. Keeping the booth in your office will not cost anything. The question is, do you have room in your office to store all the boxes and crates?

Storing the booth at the exhibit house will require you to pay a monthly storage fee. The exhibit house will also charge you a maintenance fee to reassemble the booth after the show to determine if anything needs to be cleaned or replaced.

If you consider this option, request that the exhibit house includes a separate line item for this cost in your booth purchase contract. It is easy to forget the additional costs for ongoing booth maintenance and storage when evaluating whether booth purchase or rental is the right decision.

Will you make significant changes to your marketing messages, company look and feel, strategic positioning, or product portfolio over the next year?

What are your company's strategic business plans?

While your executive management team discusses significant company changes among themselves, they may only announce their plans to the rest of the employees shortly before telling your customers and the public.

As a marketing professional working on company messaging and positioning many months in advance, you need to know in what direction the company is going over the next six months to a year so you can plan accordingly and cost-effectively.

If, for example, your company is going to rebrand itself within the next six months and the change will include new corporate colors, a new logo, and a new tagline, you may not want to spend money on a custom booth now if you will have to change everything once the rebranding is complete. In this case, rent a booth for the shows taking place in the next six months. Use that time and money to design a beautiful new booth to launch your new brand once the transition is complete.

Here are some questions to consider.

♦ Is the company moving in a different direction with a new product portfolio?

♦ Is the company moving into a new market with a new target audience? For example, transitioning from selling to lawyers to selling to teachers. Will the company's colors, logo, and messaging also change?

♦ Is the company considering purchasing another company to make your business more competitive or offer a more extensive product portfolio?

♦ Is the company interested in being sold to a larger organization?

Any significant changes to your company, its products, or strategic direction should make you think twice about your decision. Consider renting until things settle down within your organization.

Are you considering exhibiting outside of the United States?

As I told you in the introduction, the first trade show I ever managed was for a United States software company that wanted to exhibit at a technology trade show in Paris, France.

Not only was I an inexperienced exhibitor, but I had to exhibit at a trade show in a foreign country where I didn't speak the language very well, nor did I understand their shipping requirements, customs regulations, or culture.

We shipped our custom booth—and carpet—from the United States to France. Airport customs officers delayed the release of our crates, and we were required to make a cash payment to release the materials so we could install the booth on time. My stress level was through the roof.

Today, with hundreds of US and international shows behind me, exhibiting in Paris, France; London, England; Tokyo, Japan; or Rio de Janeiro, Brazil is just another show.

If you are an experienced exhibitor;
If you are exhibiting in a country where you speak the language;
If you have a specialized booth structure that requires you to ship your booth;
. . . **do it. Buy a booth.**

If you are an inexperienced exhibitor;
If you don't speak the language;
If you have a limited budget and shipping a booth from the US to another country would blow your budget out of the water;
If you have little time between a show in the United States and an international show and there is a possibility of the booth delayed in customs;
. . . **save yourself the worry and headache and rent a booth.**

While these are some of the more common considerations, there is no black and white answer to whether you should buy a custom booth or rent one. They each have their benefits and drawbacks.

Every situation is unique, and the correct answer for you may not be the right answer for another company. It requires that you understand your company's immediate and future goals.

Chapter 12: Recognize a Great Opportunity When It Presents Itself

free stuff

insider insight

Speaking

If I'd only known earlier

Once I have selected the topic on which I would like to speak, I jot down a few bullet points on the most important information I want to address in the presentation. I then write the abstract based on the primary themes on my list.

Sometimes the speaker instructions provided by show management ask you to include three to four points in your abstract submission on what attendees will learn from your presentation.

I always include information on what the attendees to my presentation will learn, whether it is requested or not.

I have two goals:

1) Get show attendees interested enough in my topic and description that they choose to come and listen to my presentation.

2) Educate, inform, enlighten, and teach those who have come to see me.

Speaking at a conference or trade show is the single most cost-effective activity with the most significant potential ROI.

I will say that again.

Speaking at a conference or trade show is the single most cost-effective activity you can participate in and a terrific way to generate quality leads, position your company as a leader in your industry, and position the speaker as a knowledge expert.

Unlike the attendees walking by your booth who may or may not have an interest in who your company is and what you do, attendees select the educational sessions they go to based on:

♦ Their interest in the subject
♦ The possibility that it might help them solve a business problem
♦ The fact that it will provide insights and information that could help them in the future

Besides the travel expense for an out-of-town event, a speaking opportunity is often free—although not always—and can provide a significant ROI. What could be better than that?

There are generally three ways in which you can speak at a trade show or conference.

Option 1: Free and open to any subject matter expert

Many shows open the opportunity to speak at their event to anyone who has expertise in the topics the show organizer has selected to focus on during the educational sessions.

You should already know the trade shows in your industry that are most important to your business. Visit each of their websites to see if they have a call for papers, call for submissions, or call for speakers, and accept speaker submissions known as abstracts. Depending on the show's size, the first request for speaker submissions could be released up to eight or nine months before the show takes place.

The speaker section of the website will include a list of topic categories chosen by the show, which will be of interest to their attendees. Select a topic or two on which you are an expert and prepare your abstract. The abstract is usually a two-paragraph overview of what you will speak about and what the attendees should expect to learn.

The selection committee may also ask you to provide a video example of a prior speaking engagement to give them a better understanding of your expertise and presentation style. The video is not usually required when submitting an abstract for a smaller or less well-known show.

These submission requirements vary from show to show, so be sure to know what the selection committee is asking for. They may throw out your submission if you do not provide what they want.

Your abstract will need to be submitted by the due date posted on the show's website. Be sure to know what that date is, and add it to your calendar. It is usually anywhere from four to seven months before the show occurs, so the selection committee has time to review the submissions and choose the speakers.

If they notify you that you or another person in your company can speak, you will have approximately two to four months to complete your presentation.

Insider insight

Before submitting an abstract for yourself or another member of your team, be sure that your proposed speaker will be able to attend. I have seen many abstracts submitted without a firm

(continued)

> *(continued)*
> commitment from the proposed speaker, and this could cause problems down the road.
>
> Some shows will allow you to substitute the speaker you originally submitted for someone else if the original speaker cannot attend.
>
> Other shows will not allow this and could eliminate your session, replacing it with another company and topic if you try to switch speakers.

Option 2: Pay-to-play

Some shows incorporate a speaking session into their exhibitor or sponsorship packages. A conference's sales department knows that you want to speak at their event, and they will include it in their sales package to entice you to spend more money on a larger booth or expensive sponsorship.

If, and only if, you are considering a specific show anyway and are interested in purchasing a booth or sponsorship because it is important to your business, then this is an excellent opportunity to get extra exposure for your company. Do not just jump at this chance to speak if it is not a show where you already see the value.

Option 3: By invitation only

For other shows, the ability to speak is by invitation only. This is frequently the case for events run by large companies in specific industries or trade organizations.

In the technology industry, where I have spent most of my career, Microsoft's Inspire event is a perfect example. Microsoft Inspire is *the* event to attend each July. Resellers, distributors, and channel partners worldwide come together to hear Microsoft's vision for the coming year, attend educational sessions, learn from other partner companies, and spark ideas for business growth. The only difference between this and other trade shows is that Microsoft invites all the speakers to participate.

Think about your industry for a moment. If you have a business relationship with the company managing the show and they have not asked you to speak at their event, call your account manager or another contact to discuss your participation with them. They may not be able to offer you your own session but may be able to add you to a panel discussion that includes other vendors, customers, or partners. Representing your business on a multi-speaker panel is undoubtedly better than not having the opportunity to speak at all.

No sales pitch

Congratulations on being selected as a speaker!

The selection committee picked you because they believe you will be able to inform and educate the show's attendees on your topic of choice.

Providing insights, advice, recommendations, and help to their participants will position you as a thought leader and encourage attendees to see you and your company as the ones with whom they should do business.

You were not selected to make your presentation an hour-long sales pitch for your products and services. Leave the hard sell at home.

Increase your presentation ROI

Presenting is a great way to position your company's speaker as a knowledge expert on a specific subject, position your company as a leader in your industry, generate qualified leads, and close them more quickly.

Conference attendees select the educational sessions they will attend based on:

♦ Their interest in the topic
♦ New opportunities for business growth
♦ The possibility that it might help them solve a business problem
♦ The chance to meet a speaker in person who they follow online

Since there are often three, four, five, or more conference presentations going on simultaneously, attendees need to choose which topic is of most interest to them or the one which they believe will provide them with the most value. Selecting your company's presentation means that they have already prequalified themselves and are a warmer potential lead than those who stop at your booth simply to throw their business card into your fishbowl, hoping to win your prize.

Use this opportunity to increase your presentation ROI. Attendee interest in your presentation is just the first step in converting them from a prospect to a customer. Be sure to qualify and convert the attendees right at the show rather than waiting to follow up with them after you have returned to your office.

How can you do this? Give them an incentive to stop by your booth and interact with your team. Include a special offer at the end of your presentation. Tell the attendees that if they stop by your booth and mention they were at the presentation, they will receive a gift or get a special discount only available to them. That will give your booth staff another opportunity to engage attendees who your presentation has already warmed up.

Chapter 13:
Have Your Cake
and Eat It Too

Trade Publication Circulation

If I'd only known earlier

The readership of trade magazines, websites, newspapers, and other publications will surge during a trade show, especially for those publications that have chosen to be media sponsors or are allowed to distribute their magazine free of charge to show attendees.

This added readership is a perfect opportunity for you to expose your company to hundreds, thousands, or tens of thousands of additional potential buyers.

Whether it's agriculture, financial services, tourism, or manufacturing, every industry has magazines or newspapers focused on telling that industry's stories.

In the automotive industry, for example, six of the most popular US automotive magazines are *Car and Driver*, *Motor Trend*, *Hot Rod*, *Road & Track*, *Automobile*, and *Autoweek*.

Publications like these often partner with industry trade shows, such as the North American International Auto Show, to write about the educational sessions, exhibiting companies, and industry trends.

They can significantly increase their readership during this time by making free copies available to all attendees.

This often adding another 1,000, 5,000, 10,000, 20,000, or more readers to the average circulation.

The hope is that attendees exposed to a magazine at the show will like it enough to become paying subscribers. These new subscribers are beneficial for the magazine because they increase the paid circulation and benefit the trade show since the event receives a great deal of free press coverage.

In addition to the magazine issues distributed at the show, the trade show also produces a *Show Daily*. This publication, either in print, online, or both, is produced each day of the show and features articles about exhibitors, their products and services, educational presentations, c-level interviews, special guests, keynote speakers, and other exciting show activities.

Learning which publications will participate in the show can provide your company with free press and a larger potential sales footprint.

Step 1

Visit the trade show's website to find the list of participating publications. Depending on the site's layout, you may have to dig a bit to find the information. Pages like *media sponsors* or *media partners* will include this information. If that is not available, look at the exhibitor list. A magazine that is also exhibiting will be included on the exhibitor list.

If you already signed an exhibitor contract and you receive a preregistered attendee list, you may find the media publications on this list.

Lastly, you can also reach out to the show's public relations (PR) contact and request a list of media outlets and contacts to whom they have given press credentials.

Step 2

Once you uncover the publications' names, visit each of their websites to review their media kit. A media kit is a PDF document or collection of documents that provide information on each publication's:

- ♦ Reader and subscriber circulation numbers for their print and online issues
- ♦ Reader demographics
- ♦ Advertising rates, production requirements, and deadlines
- ♦ Editorial policy, feature stories, and general topics to be written about in future issues. This document is an editorial calendar.

The primary focus of a media kit is to convince a business to advertise. While you can certainly choose to spend money on advertising, we're focusing here on free editorial opportunities.

The media kit's editorial component, as its name implies, includes the editorial calendar showing each of the publication's release dates (monthly, biweekly, or weekly), deadline, editorial focus, and information on each issue's feature story. If you are lucky, it may also include reporter names and the specific topics on which they will be writing.

Your objective is to determine which issue they will distribute when your show occurs, and the topics covered.

Let's suppose that your company is in the automotive industry, and you plan to announce the release of your company's new aftermarket air induction system at the upcoming North American International Auto Show. Knowing that one of the automotive publications will have additional circulation at the show and their show issue will focus on aftermarket products should motivate you to contact the magazine to gauge their interest in learning about your product and publishing your press release.

Step 3

Now that I've given you an automotive industry example, let's think about real-life media opportunities for your company. Think about your company's industry, the show in which you will be exhibiting, and the publications that will be at the show.

Here are some opportunities you may be able to take advantage of:

♦ If you will launch a new product or service during the show, be sure to write a press release announcing your launch. Send the release to the publication. They may include it in a new product announcement or industry news section of their print and online issues.

♦ Visit the publication's website looking for articles similar to your company's area of expertise and the products and services you sell. Jot down the names of the reporters and journalists who write those articles. Reach out to these people to introduce your company, and invite them to stop by your booth during the show to learn more.

♦ If you know one of the reporters is already researching a story that will appear in the publication's show issue or on their website, reach out to them and suggest an interview of your CEO or another member of your management team. Your CEO may offer a contrarian opinion to those people already interviewed, or present insights understood only by industry leaders like him or her.

♦ If a reporter's schedule is already full during show hours, offer to take them to dinner or invite them to your evening networking reception.

♦ If a member of your management team is speaking during an educational track, invite the reporter to learn more about the topic and personally meet the speaker after the presentation.

♦ If you can demonstrate your expertise on a subject of interest to the publication, offer to write and submit an article for inclusion in their show issue. While the publication may or may not allow an outsider to publish an article in their print magazine, media outlets are always looking for well-written articles for their website.

Postscript

In addition to the opportunities I already described, there are trade publications with a pay-to-play policy. They will allow you to write and publish an article in their magazine if you purchase advertising.

I intentionally chose not to discuss that in this chapter since I want to take this time to tell you about free media opportunities that you could benefit from and wouldn't drain your budget.

If you are interested in having a presence in a publication that requires you to place an ad, you will need to weigh the potential media ROI and increase in sales vs. the advertising cost.

I am not saying that you should or should not pay for ad space to receive editorial coverage. In my career, I have done both. I have worked hard to secure free opportunities such as booth meetings, product demonstrations, and senior-level interviews for most of the shows in which I have exhibited.

In a few cases, I have paid for advertising to receive editorial coverage. Based on the publications' focus, subscriber demographics, circulation, and other criteria, combined with our company goals, the cost was worth the return.

You must make this decision for your organization.

Chapter 14: The Good Publicity Hound

Public Relations

Public relations increases your trade show participation value exponentially by exposing your company to new groups of potential customers, employees, and investors. It doesn't hurt that it is also a free opportunity.

Public relations and media coverage:

♦ Increase awareness of your company by show attendees and other exhibitors, boosting the flow of traffic to your booth.

♦ Increase awareness of your company and products to potential customers who have not attended the event.

♦ Provide exposure through both print and online trade publications, video, television, and other media.

♦ Enable you to meet and interact personally with various journalists, bloggers, and reporters with whom you may have never been able to connect through emails or phone calls outside of the show.

E very show includes some press members, whether they are reporters, bloggers, analysts, or other industry influencers. They attend to check out what is new and different on the topics in which they write.

You can access the list of registered members of the press by requesting a media list from show management or the show's public relations department. It will be easier and quicker for you to request a preregistered media list of contact names and publications once your company has become an official show exhibitor.

If you are unable to get a media list from show management or their PR department, you should be able to compile your own list by reviewing the preregistered attendee list that you may have received when signing your exhibitor contract. If you are familiar with many of your industry's trade publications or news websites, look through the attendee list to discover the reporters, journalists, and bloggers from those publications and sites.

There is no cost to receive and use this media list. Reporters who preregister for the show know their contact information will appear on the list, and exhibitors will contact them about upcoming product launches, on-site interview requests, or in-booth product demonstrations.

Other shows set up a unique online portal where attendees and exhibitors can network and schedule show-based meetings. Take advantage of this terrific opportunity and reach out to reporters whom you feel would be interested in learning more about what your company is doing, new product announcements, a sneak peek at new technologies, and more.

Various PR opportunities

PR is not simply about securing an interview and having a feature article about your company appear in your industry's most well-known trade magazine. There are many different types of PR opportunities.

Online and print exhibitor listing

Every trade show creates a guide that includes presentation times and locations, a convention center or conference facility map, the expo hall floor plan, and a listing of all exhibitors with their contact information, booth number, company logo, description, and special booth events. This information will be available on the show's website, a specially created show app, or in print.

A basic exhibitor listing is free. That's right; it's free. So be sure to fill your company listing with an exciting description to entice people to stop by your booth. Both attendees and the press review this guide to learn more about exhibitors and determine which booths they will visit first.

Should you want to add more information than you can fit in the free listing, you can include it for a fee.

Press kit/media kit distribution

A press kit or media kit is a packet of information that gives a reporter the information they need to learn about your company, its value proposition, and products so they can quickly write a short article, blog post, or other stories. It will also help them determine their level of interest in reaching out to you to conduct a more in-depth interview.

A press kit includes many of the following items, but you can customize it to your company's needs.

♦ *Company overview*. Describe what your company does, the products and services you offer, the types of customers you serve, and what differentiates you from your competitors. A company overview includes a history of how the organization grew into the business it is today. It may also report on significant acquisitions that have occurred over the years and changes in executive management.

♦ *Fact sheet.* The fact sheet is a less in-depth one-page overview of the company with a simple bulleted list used to relay key milestones, awards, customer growth, and other essential facts that have occurred over the years. It is a quick snapshot of key company statistics.

♦ *Biographies.* These are short biographies of the executive management team. It may include one or more biographies of the company's CEO, president, founder, chairman, or other notable employees.

♦ *Product collateral or one-page descriptive overview.* This includes sales collateral or a one-page overview for a new product launch. It may also include targeted products or services for a reporter interested in learning more about your offering, its capabilities, and benefits.

♦ *Photographs, videos, or other multimedia elements.* This includes high-resolution photos of the company CEO, products, and corporate headquarters, as well as a file of your company logo. These materials enable a reporter to write a story or repost a press release without having to spend time requesting and waiting for you to send materials.

♦ *Customer quotes and testimonials.* This includes a printed list of customer quotes or a video file of their thoughts on your company, products they have purchased from you, and whether they would recommend others purchase your services as well.

♦ *Recent press releases.* Include a copy of any press release you distributed in the last six months.

- *Recent press coverage.* Include print copies, pdf files, or videos of recent press coverage your company has received in newspapers, trade magazines, television shows, or news reports.
- *PR contact information.* Include the name, email address, and phone number of your company's public relations contact as well as contact information for a PR agency who may be supporting you during the show or is your PR agency of record.
- *Quarterly financials or an annual report.* If your organization is a public company, you may decide to include a copy of the last quarter's financial statement or a copy of the current year's annual report.

Traditionally, all components of a company's media kit would be assembled at your office, shipped to the show, and brought to the press room, where they were made available to any member of the media interested in your news.

While this is still the way you distribute a press kit at small, less tech-based trade shows or conferences, many of today's large, tech-friendly shows create an online media portal. Exhibitors can securely post their press kit in an electronic format for easy and convenient download by reporters before, during, and after the show.

Turn to the next chapter to better understand the format a press release and media alert should take.

Editorial mention in the *Show Daily*

As discussed in chapter 13, the *Show Daily* is the show's official publication. It covers show news, new product announcements, exhibitor interviews, industry trends, and more.

A new issue of the *Show Daily* is published each day and can be printed, published online, or both.

An electronic pre-show edition is also published to get attendees excited for what they will see and learn at the show, and a post-show edition is published as a show wrap-up.

Exhibitors can submit press releases and company news for inclusion in the *Show Daily*. There is no charge to be included.

New product launch announcements are of particular interest to the media and show attendees, and a product press release has a high probability of being included for free.

Consider that distributing a product launch press release a month before or a month after your show takes place may result in 0.05 percent of the show's attendees seeing the announcement in industry media. Those who do see the announcement may intend to visit your website and learn more but rarely get to your site because they are busy in their office with other work to do.

Ten, 20, 30, 40, or 50 percent more potential customers will see your new product announcement if you submit it for inclusion in the *Show Daily*. These people are already at the show, so jotting down your booth number and stopping by your booth will be easy.

Daily events schedule

Each edition of the *Show Daily* includes a schedule of events for that day. It might consist of sponsored receptions, an expo hall cocktail hour, keynote presentations by notable speakers, book signings, special giveaways, and other not-to-be-missed events.

Did your CEO write a book?

Do you want to hold a book signing in your booth?

Write a press release announcing the book's release and when and where the signing will take place. Be sure that the *Show Daily*'s editor receives a copy of the release approximately a week before the show takes place so they can add the information to their calendar of events.

Interview requests and meet and greets

Invite a reporter, journalist, or blogger to your booth, to an after-hours networking event, a reception, or even just a cup of coffee. It does not need to be a formal sit-down interview, with the outcome being an article posted the next day—although that would be great.

Introduce them to your team, your products, and your company, explaining how you are a leader or innovator in your industry and what makes you different. Offer to be available to them whenever they have general questions about the industry or are looking for an alternative opinion when writing about a topic on which you are an expert.

Meeting in person at the show may or may not garner immediate press, but, more importantly, it can lay the groundwork for long-term relationships and many future media opportunities to come.

On-site press room or media center

An on-site press room or media center has three primary purposes:

♦ Exhibitors can drop off press kits and other company materials they would like to provide to the media. The kits are free for any reporter, editor, blogger, or another journalist to take if they are interested in your company, your product offering, your area of expertise, or your market.

♦ A reporter can interview an exhibitor in this quieter, out-of-the-way location. Exhibitors cannot use the press room on their own, but you can use this space with a member of the media.

♦ The press can use this room on their own to write stories about what they have seen and experienced at the show.

Press conference

A press conference is a great way to attract media attention if you plan to announce a new product release, show sponsorship, business partnership, award, or other activity related to your participation.

You should be able to reserve space in the press room/media room, in your exhibitor booth, or possibly in other areas of the convention center, conference center, or hotel. You should also write a media alert for this event and make sure you submit it for inclusion in the *Show Daily*'s event schedule.

Ask the show's PR department if they will give you a preregistered list of all media members who will be attending the show. At a minimum, be sure these media contacts receive a copy of your announcement. You may also want to personally invite each of them to your press conference.

Press conference space is usually available on a first-come, first-served basis, so be sure to reach out to the show's media or PR team as far in advance of the show as you can to ensure a room is available.

Chapter 15:
For Immediate Release
Press Releases and Media Alerts

If I'd only known earlier

Are you speaking at an upcoming show? Will you launch a new product? Let people know.

Write and distribute a press release three to four weeks before the show takes place. The announcement will generate additional pre-show interest and enable attendees to add your activities to their calendar of things to do. It will assist in online marketing efforts by having your information appear when someone searches for a particular show.

But don't stop there. Write and distribute a media alert one week before the show begins highlighting a specific activity you will participate in or something you will feature in your booth. Many reporters, bloggers, and others watch for these announcements and may reach out to you for a larger story—or at least stop by your booth to learn more.

The *Show Daily*, which includes a wrap-up of what happened at the show on the previous day and previews what will happen at the show on that day, may publish your alert, resulting in additional attendee traffic to your booth or speaker session.

What is the difference between a press release and a media alert or media advisory? A press release is a formal announcement of news that a company or organization wants to distribute to the press.

You can write a press release to publicize a new product launch, company acquisition, business partnership, new employee, and other newsworthy information.

A standard press release format includes a headline, subhead, opening paragraph, at least one quote, a company boilerplate, and primary business contact. The average length of a press release is approximately 650 words.

Your goal is to get editors to publish your news in their publication and, possibly, have a journalist reach out to schedule a formal interview.

Since a press release is a public announcement, you should release it on the day you wish to make your information public.

For example, let's say you want to announce a new product launch on March 1, which is also the show's opening day. The press release date should be dated March 1, and the release should be distributed to the media on March 1 via a press release distribution service. Examples include Business Wire, EIN Presswire, PR Newswire, and PRWeb, but there are others.

Here is a sample of a fictional press release I wrote that announces a speaker session from an exhibiting firm. This announcement follows the format of a standard press release.

FOR IMMEDIATE RELEASE

Bridgeton CEO to Speak at SaaS NOW Spring Conference

Andrew Turner will discuss ten competitive advantages of market segmentation, which you can implement today to blow away your competition.

BOSTON, MA - February 2, 2022 - Bridgeton, LLC, the leading provider of SaaS-based marketing segmentation software, ColorMe Purple, announced today that the Company's CEO, Andrew Turner, will be speaking at the SaaS NOW Spring Conference and Expo.

SaaS NOW Conference and Expo will be held at the Ernest N. Morial Convention Center in New Orleans, Louisiana, from April 6–8, 2022. The event brings together small and mid-size companies and large enterprises across all industries to whom SaaS-based business productivity and collaboration software is critical for the day-to-day management of their organization and future growth. This year's conference is expected to welcome 20,000 attendees worldwide.

Mr. Turner will speak to attendees on Wednesday, April 7, 2022. His presentation titled "Ten Competitive Advantages of Market Segmentation You Can Implement Today to Blow Away Your Competition" will demonstrate the advantages of market segmentation as a marketing strategy, the foundational element of market segmentation, and how it can be a significant competitive advantage.

"B2B customers frequently select a vendor based on how well the vendor understands the customer's business needs and whether they believe the business can help them meet their objectives or eliminate their pain," said Andrew Turner, Bridgeton CEO. "Since 60 percent of businesses are still taking the spray-and-pray marketing approach, you can realize an immediate advantage over your competitors by implementing segmentation as a foundational element of your marketing strategy."

Bridgeton, LLC maintains its competitive advantage in a crowded martech marketplace by offering its full-service ColorMe Purple SaaS solution as a private label service to marketing agencies across the United States. The private label capability enables agencies to sell the solution to their clients under their own brand, providing a differentiated suite of marketing services and an additional revenue stream.

In addition to the Company's presentation, Bridgeton will demonstrate its ColorMe Purple SaaS-based segmentation and analytics tools at the Company's booth #1142 in Expo Hall A.

About Bridgeton, LLC
Bridgeton is a leading provider of cloud marketing services that segments and analyzes customer data. SMB and enterprise companies across all industries benefit from the company's ColorMe Purple SaaS service by driving more significant levels of sales and marketing differentiation, revenue growth, and

profitability. ColorMe Purple is also available as a white-label service to marketing agencies to implement in minutes. An uptime guarantee and live support are provided to all customers. To learn more, please visit https://www.bridgeton.net.

###

Contact:
Sarah Collins
Bridgeton, LLC
555-207-0475
scollins@bridgeton.net

Unlike a press release, a media alert or media advisory is a brief one-page bulletin used to provide the Who, What, Where, and When, of an event, press conference, speaker presentation, or other activity. It simply reports the facts. It does not contain quotes or more descriptive language that you find in a press release.

A media alert can be distributed to a targeted list of media contacts five or more days before the event occurs.

Reporters, editors, television and radio producers, and other contacts who write about topics related to your industry, your company, and the products you sell should be on that list.

The goal is to:

♦ Get the media contacts to attend your event or activity.
♦ Encourage media contacts to share this information with their audience.
♦ Increase attendance at your event.

Here is a media alert sample that provides more detailed information on the Bridgeton CEO's speaker session at the SaaS NOW Spring Conference and Expo.

Andrew Turner, Bridgeton CEO to Present Educational Session, "Ten Competitive Advantages of Market Segmentation You Can Implement Today to Blow Away Your Competition, " at the SaaS NOW Spring Conference and Expo.

WHO: Bridgeton, LLC is a leading provider of cloud marketing services, which segments and analyzes customer data. Small business and enterprise customers across all industries benefit from the Company's ColorMe Purple SaaS service by driving more significant sales and marketing differentiation, revenue growth, and profitability.

WHAT: Educational Session—"Ten Competitive Advantages of Market Segmentation You Can Implement Today to Blow Away Your Competition."
Presented by: Andrew Turner, CEO, Bridgeton, LLC

Potential business-to-business customers evaluate your products and services based on how well you understand their business needs and goals and whether they believe you can help them meet their objectives. Demonstrating your understanding of customer needs requires you to segment your messaging, marketing materials, and sales channels to ensure you speak their language. Market segmentation should be a fundamental element of your marketing strategy and can be a significant competitive advantage. We'll take a deep dive into ten components of market segmentation you can implement today to blow away your competition.

WHERE: Ernest N. Morial Convention Center
900 Convention Center Blvd., New Orleans, LA 70130
Bridgeton Booth #1142, Expo Hall A

WHEN: SaaS NOW Conference and Expo
April 6–8, 2022

Educational Session
April 7, 2022
Palm Court Terrace D
10:30-11:30 a.m.

To register for the conference, please visit https://www.saasnowconf.co.

For details on Bridgeton's full line of products, services, and solutions, please visit us at https://www.bridgeton.net.

About Bridgeton, LLC

Bridgeton is a leading provider of cloud marketing services that segments and analyzes customer data. SMB and enterprise companies across all industries benefit from the company's ColorMe Purple SaaS service by driving more significant levels of sales and marketing differentiation, revenue growth, and profitability. ColorMe Purple is also available as a white-label service to marketing agencies to implement in minutes. An uptime guarantee and live support provided to all customers. To learn more, please visit https://www.bridgeton.net.

###

Contact:
Sarah Collins
Bridgeton, LLC
555-207-0475
scollins@bridgeton.net

Using my press release and media alert as examples, think about what announcements would benefit your business.

Chapter 16:
A Journey of 1,000 Miles Begins With the Right Shipper

Shipping Options

If I'd only known earlier

You have many shipping options. Personal car. Freight carrier. Commercial airline. Private trucking company.

If you have no experience shipping a large booth, you may want to use the show-approved shipping company to ensure that your booth will arrive on time and, hopefully, in good condition. They are specialists in shipping trade show booths, and they already know the rules and regulations of the show and the convention center in which it is taking place.

Your exhibitor services manual should include the name of the show's recommended freight handling company.

I am only mentioning this as a convenient option for you if you are inexperienced with trade show shipping ins and outs. You are under no obligation to use the show-approved shipper. You can select any company and shipping option you wish.

W hether you have a small 10 x 10 ft. pop-up booth that fits into two sturdy black plastic-wheeled cases or a larger 40 x

50 ft. booth that requires five custom-built crates, you have options as to how you get your booth, graphics, and other materials to and from a trade show.

How you ship your booth may change from show to show and will most likely be determined by one or more of four criteria:

- ♦ Your trade show budget and the amount of that budget you have allocated for shipping
- ♦ The amount of time you have to get your booth and other materials to the show
- ♦ The distance between your office and the show
- ♦ How fragile your show materials are

For example, a business in Boston, Massachusetts, that is exhibiting in a 10 x 20 ft. booth at its first show in New York City may decide to ship their booth structure through a common carrier like FedEx or UPS.

However, they will send their fragile glass display items in the car of one of their staff who will drive the 206 miles from their home in Boston to the Javits Center in Manhattan.

A 30 x 40 ft. island booth picked up from two separate locations in Dallas, Texas, traveling to the Moscone Center in San Francisco, California, with only two days to get there will most certainly be shipped using an air freight company.

Here are the shipping options you will need to consider:

Deliver by car

Transporting your booth in your car to a show within driving distance is a no-brainer.

However, it is essential to fully understand the specific rules that show management puts in place to restrict the types of materials you, as an exhibitor or another member of your team, can physically bring into the hall yourself. I'll discuss this further in a minute.

Ship as luggage

If you have a 10 x 10 ft. booth that can fit into one or two of those wheeled plastic cases that I previously mentioned and you are flying to the show, you can bring both cases with you to the airport and check them as luggage.

Of course, there will be a cost to do this. But, if you have a limited budget, the price is certainly nowhere near what it would be to have a trucking company transport your cases.

Insider insight

Selecting the *delivery by car* or *ship as luggage* option means that you will be schlepping your cases around with you.

Do you want to do that? Can you do that?

Exhibitors often select these options if they want to eliminate or significantly reduce their shipping and drayage expenses.

As I will discuss in greater detail in chapter 20, drayage refers to your booth materials' movement from the expo hall's loading dock to your booth space and the movement of your materials back to the loading dock when the show is over.

While driving your booth to the show in your car will eliminate the shipping expense and shipping it as luggage will reduce your shipping expense, you still have the drayage hurdle to overcome once you arrive at the convention center.

The rules and regulations of every convention center or conference center are different. Be sure to read your exhibitor services manual carefully.

(continued)

(continued)

Does it mention hand carriable items? You need to know.

It's important to understand your choices, but it's more important to understand the consequences of not following the show's rules.

Whether you choose to deliver by car or ship as luggage, this is an important point to know

Exhibiting companies looking to save money often instruct employees to bring the booth materials into the convention center themselves.

This action circumvents the union labor and attempts to eliminate material handling and drayage costs—more about that later. If this is a strategy that you are considering, be careful.

Open your exhibitor services manual to the material handling information section and see if there is a paragraph that discusses how to hand carry show materials to your booth.

A hand-carriable item is defined as an item you can carry into and out of the expo hall unassisted. If your booth structure, graphics, literature, tchotchkes, and other materials are packed into a couple of portable cases that you can easily carry or push into the hall yourself, then you should be all set.

If you require a dolly or four-wheeled cart to bring your booth to your space in the hall, the official show contractor or union representative may stop you as you enter. They know your objective is to eliminate the drayage charge, so they may ask you to turn over your boxes to the convention center staff. They will then charge you the drayage fee for a union laborer to deliver the materials to your booth space.

Common carriers

Shipping your booth via a well-known carrier such as UPS, FedEx, or DHL is an intermediate option.

Using one of these companies to send your booth and materials will be more expensive than hand-carrying your items but will still be less expensive than a private trucking or freight transport company.

Benefit: Since these companies provide tracking information, you will be able to track your shipment every step of the way. If your time is limited, they can get your shipment to its destination quickly.

Drawback: Your shipment will most likely not be sent directly from its pickup location to its destination without stops in between. A carrier will deliver it to their hub in a specific city.

The shipment will be consolidated with other cargo and transferred to another plane or truck going to your destination. Each time your shipment stops at a sorting facility or transfers to another vehicle, you run the risk of damage or loss.

Private trucking or freight handling companies

A 10 x 20 ft. or larger booth with multiple crates and pallets of boxes will require a trucking/van line or freight handling company.

Benefit: A van line or trucking company specializing in the shipment of large trade show booths will be more knowledgeable and sensitive to how your materials are secured and handled en route. It will also ship your booth directly to the show location with little or no stops in various hubs along the way.

Drawback: This can be one of the more expensive options.

You are free to select whichever shipping company you like. However, if an exhibit house built your booth, ask them to recommend a reputable shipper that their clients have used in the past.

An exhibit house specializing in building booths for companies in a specific industry may have multiple clients exhibiting at a particular show. In that case, they can consolidate all the shipments going to the advance warehouse or direct to the convention center. Since all the shipments are destined for the same place, this can save you money and time.

Suppose you are exhibiting at the International Builder's Show in Las Vegas and your exhibit house has five clients all exhibiting at that show. The exhibit house can work with you, the other clients, and their preferred van line to load six booths worth of materials onto four trucks and send them directly to Las Vegas.

In addition to deciding which shipment method you will use, you need to determine if you will ship to the show's advance warehouse or direct to the convention center or conference center.

Shipping to the advance warehouse

Your booth materials can be shipped to the advance warehouse up to a month before the show takes place. The shipping section of your exhibitor services manual will tell you the first and last day that materials can arrive at the advance warehouse.

Shipping to the advance warehouse rather than directly to the hall is one of those items that can save you 20–40 percent. It also ensures that show staff will deliver your shipment to your booth space before your target installation time begins, enabling you and your team to start your booth's installation without delay.

Shipping to the convention or conference center

Suppose you cannot complete your booth's construction or print your product literature before the advance warehouse deadline. In that case, you will need to ship them directly to the convention center.

If this is the situation you find yourself in, please heed the following advice. It will eliminate a lot of unnecessary stress for you.

Know your target date and time

Show management gives each exhibitor a target move-in or installation date and time. This enables them to maintain an orderly flow of freight by staggering delivery dates and times based on your booth's location in the hall and any custom requirements you may have.

Any freight you had shipped to the advance warehouse over the previous month will be brought to the hall by show staff and delivered to your booth space by your scheduled target time.

If your freight handling company or van line delivers your booth directly to the expo hall, you should provide them with your target date and time. A target time of 8:30–10:30 a.m. on Monday means that the show staff is prepared to accept your shipment during that time. Instruct your shipping provider to arrive at the show's marshaling yard before your target time—in this example, 8:30 a.m.—so they are sure to be unloaded at some point during the target time.

The marshaling yard is a parking lot, freight yard, or other location where all trucks carrying exhibitor freight check-in. They then wait their turn to be called to the trade show facility's dock for unloading. This process ensures freight arrives at the hall in an orderly way and there are no roadblocks or traffic jams around the convention center, conference center, or hotel.

Suppose your freight handling company arrives at the marshaling yard after the target time. This late start will significantly delay your ability to install your booth, and you will incur extra material handling charges.

Insider insight

To ensure that the team you have hired to install your booth isn't standing around waiting for your booth structure to be delivered, make certain the installation time you select is after your target time.

If you hand-carry your booth into the hall, the target time does not apply to you. You may enter the hall on your target date as soon as the doors open.

Chapter 17: When Cheaper Isn't Better

Reserve Your Hotel

If I'd only known earlier

If the hotel reservation page on the trade show's website says, "no more discounted rooms are available," call the show hotel directly.

A show hotel sets aside a percentage of its rooms for show attendees. Hotels catering to big shows with tens of thousands of attendees like the RSA Conference, E3, InfoComm, MAGIC, or the National Restaurant Association Show may allocate all rooms for show visitors because they attract so many attendees that there is enormous demand. If this is the case, you could be out of luck trying to get into that hotel.

Other hotels often set aside a large percentage of their rooms for show attendees but leave some rooms available for non-event customers who come into town for different reasons.

So, even though the web page says there are no more discounted rooms available for show participants, there may still be rooms available, just not at the discounted rate.

(continued)

(continued)

See if you can reserve a room directly on the hotel's website or call their direct reservation line.

W hether your trade show, expo, or conference is in a convention center, a conference center, or other location, there is sure to be a hotel next to or in close walking distance of the facility, which is the *show hotel*.

A hotel receives this distinction when the show's management team arranges with them to set aside a large block of rooms at a discounted price for people coming into town specifically for that show.

I have exhibited at smaller conferences where all events and activities take place in this one hotel. That includes the exhibit space, educational presentations, after-hours networking events, and all the sleeping rooms.

I have also presented at conferences where the expo hall, educational presentations, and speaker sleeping rooms are in the show hotel. Then three other hotels in the area are selected to house the attendees.

Whether show management selects one or more hotels as the show hotel depends on the show's size, facilities required, and the number of rooms available.

Monitor the reservation instructions and deadline

As soon as you have confirmed your participation in a particular show, visit the show's website. It will include a page of information about the show hotel.

The instructions may enable you to make a reservation directly on the show's website. More likely, it will include a link to a unique landing page on the hotel's website. The page will be accessible by exhibitors, speakers, and attendees only and will enable you to reserve discounted rooms on a first-come, first-served basis.

As you put together your list of attendees and booth duty staff, be sure to keep the hotel reservation deadline top of mind. Once the deadline has passed, any unreserved rooms will be released to the public at the full hotel room rate.

This assumes there are still rooms available.

Insider insight

For popular trade shows like the marketing industry's Inbound Conference or technology vendor shows like Microsoft's Inspire Conference, don't wait until the day before the hotel's deadline to reserve your room.

Hotel rooms at popular shows with 10,000, 30,000, 50,000, or more attendees may fill up months before the show occurs. As soon as your booth staff list is complete, make the hotel reservations.

If you don't make the hotel reservations ASAP, you may visit the show's website and find a message that says,

No more discounted rooms are available. Please check other hotels in the area to reserve a room.

Don't necessarily reject the full room rate

I can remember a few times in my trade show career when the show hotel's discounted rooms were no longer available because we waited too long to decide whether we would participate.

The discounted room rate may have been $150 per night, but since the deadline had passed, our only option was to pay the standard room price of $200 or $225.

Inevitably, my boss would then dismiss the show hotel as too expensive and select a less expensive hotel three or four miles from the convention center.

With decades of experience comes additional insight.

My recommendation is that even if the show hotel is now charging its standard full room rate, don't reject that hotel out of hand because you believe the price is too high.

Consider the implications of staying in a hotel fifty, seventy-five, or even one hundred dollars less than the show hotel next to the convention center, but it is located a few miles down the road.

Let's look at an example of hotel options for a show taking place at the Las Vegas Convention Center in Las Vegas, Nevada.

The discounted rooms at the show hotel are already booked by other attendees, but they still have a few rooms available at the standard room rate.

You must now decide whether you should book a room in the show hotel at their standard room rate or consider an optional hotel on the Las Vegas strip that is farther away but less expensive.

Show dates: September 27–30
Arrival date: September 26
Departure date: October 1

Show location: Las Vegas Convention Center

Show hotel: Residence Inn Las Vegas Convention Center
Optional hotel: Mandalay Bay Resort and Casino

TABLE 8. Cost and time comparison of show hotel vs. another hotel option

	Show hotel discount rate	Show hotel standard rate	Optional hotel standard rate
Room rate Five nights plus taxes and fees).	$1,220.00	$1,495.00	$1,034.00
Distance to Las Vegas Convention Center	0.3-mile walk	0.3-mile walk	5.7-mile drive
Taxi fare Four trips per day to and from hotel and convention center. Includes 20 percent tip. Five days. $21.48/trip.	—	—	$515.60
Travel time Four trips per day to and from hotel and convention center for five days.	1 hour, 19 minutes	1 hour, 19 minutes	3 hours, 19 minutes
Total cost	$1,220.00	$1,495.00	$1,549.60
Total travel time	1 hour, 19 minutes	1 hour, 19 minutes	3 hours, 19 minutes

When trying to decide whether to stay at the show hotel for a standard rate or another hotel a distance away, you may jump at the Mandalay Bay reservation because the cost is $461.00 less than the standard room rate at the Residence Inn. That would seem like the common-sense thing to do. But consider this ...

At a minimum, you will be traveling:

♦ From your hotel to the convention center in the morning

- From the convention center to your hotel to freshen up after the show is over for the day
- From the hotel back to the convention center or show hotel in the evening for networking receptions or parties
- Back to your hotel at the end of the night

That requires a minimum of four trips back and forth.

You will be able to walk between the Marriott Residence Inn show hotel and the convention center, so it won't cost any money.

If you stay at Mandalay Bay, you will need to travel by car.

In this example, let's take a taxi. Four trips in a cab each day for five days plus a 20 percent tip each time will cost you $515.60.

You must also consider what your time is worth. Since you can walk between the Marriott and the convention center, the total travel time to go back and forth over the five days will be approximately one hour and nineteen minutes.

Since you will need to take a car between Mandalay Bay and the convention center, the total travel time will be about three hours and nineteen minutes.

Yes, staying at another hotel a distance from the convention center will save you money. In this case, staying at Mandalay Bay will save you $461.00 over the show hotel at their standard room rate. But, when you add in the travel time and expense, you will end up paying $54.60 more to stay at a hotel five miles down the road and waste more time getting there.

How does this compare to your situation?

Think about the specific needs of you and your team.

How will your decision impact your team's productivity, efficiency, and effectiveness?

- How long will it take you to get from the less expensive hotel to the convention center and back again? If your show is in a city like New York or Los Angeles, even a distance of a couple of miles could take you a full thirty to forty-five minutes to get from one location to the other due to the traffic.
- How are you going to make the trip? Will you get an Uber or Lyft, rent a car, take a taxi, or hop on the subway? These transportation options all cost money.
- If you have asked a new customer to stop by your booth at 1:00 p.m. to sign a sales contract, but you left the contract in your hotel room five miles away, will you have enough time to get to your hotel and back again before the customer shows up?
- Networking events typically run late into the evening. If you are attending an event that ends at 11:30 p.m., will transportation be available for you to get back to your hotel?

Each of these scenarios is real. They can happen.

You know the full room rate that you will have to pay at the show hotel. Think about the city in which the show is taking place, the distance from a less expensive hotel to the convention center, the time it will take you to get there, the transportation options available to you, and the cost that each person will incur to travel back and forth.

You may find that spending $225 per person at the show hotel rather than $150 at the less expensive hotel is offset by the transportation cost savings of walking to the convention center as well as the increased convenience and flexibility it provides.

I am not trying to steer you one way or another. You should make this decision.

Each company's needs and requirements are unique, and you know what is best for your team. I'm just offering options and providing alternative ways of thinking.

The final decision is yours.

Chapter 18: Don't Waste My Time

save time

Coordinating On-Site Vendors

If I'd only known earlier

When planning for booth assembly, you must think about each item to be installed, the contractor who will install it, and the order in which the contractors must do their work.

Each contractor is responsible for a different component of your booth's installation. One element of the installation builds on the next. For example, the furniture rental contractor should deliver the couch and armchairs after the show contractor installs the carpet, not before.

If you have a 30 x 30 ft. island booth with a large demo station in the middle, you must run electricity to the kiosk to power the demo station before installing the carpet. You can't run extension cords across your booth on top of the carpet. It will be rather ugly, and booth visitors could trip over your cords.

Early in my marketing career, I remember exhibiting at a technology show at the Orange County Convention Center in Orlando, Florida. I asked my team member to fax all the service request forms to the show decorator's office. While my team member sent the paperwork to their office, she did not follow up to confirm that the corresponding vendors, such as electrical, furniture rental, and booth installation, actually *received* the paperwork.

This lack of follow-up caused a bit of a problem when I arrived at the hall during booth installation.

One-inch foam padding installed? . . . Check.

Dark gray carpet installed? . . . Check.

Show contractor on-site at booth location? . . . Check.

Booth installation in process? . . . Check.

As I checked each component off in my head, I realized one critical element was missing. Can you spot it as you look through my list?

The electrical service is missing. This meant that the contractor had not run electricity to our two demo kiosks and our center tower displaying unlit graphics.

I was upset and nervous at the same time. I ran to the show's electrical desk to determine what happened. The electrical manager said they never received our order form. After I completed a new form at the desk, he said they would stop by our booth within four hours to install the electricity.

Now what was I going to do?

The carpet was already on the floor, and thousands of pounds of booth structure was already standing on top of it. We decided that extension cords would have to be run on top of the gray carpet and taped down so no booth staff member or trade show attendee would trip over the cords. The addition of unsightly cords taped to our carpet was certainly not how I wanted our booth to look. Nor did I want anyone to be hurt.

Two fundamental lessons came from that trade show in Orlando. First, confirm via phone or email that the show decorator or third-party vendors have received all service request forms. Second, there is a specific order in which you should install services and fixtures to ensure the booth operates correctly, is visually appealing, and everyone is safe.

Take a lesson from my trade show ordeal

Suppose your next show is in Chicago, Illinois, and that the general show contractor is called Contractor A.

Let's look at all the different elements on the completion list and the number of different companies supplying the services.

TABLE 9. Items to be completed or services installed and various associated contractors

	Contractor
Booth structure and exhibitor materials brought to your booth space	Contractor A
Show contracted labor to install booth structure	Contractor A
Carpet rental and installation	Contractor A
Rigging rental and contracted labor to hang your company sign from ceiling	Contractor A
In-booth internet service	Contractor B
Furniture rental	Contractor A
Electrical installation	Contractor A
Lead capture device rental	Contractor C
Photography services	Contractor D
Automotive detailing for in-booth car display	Contractor E

Strategically coordinating the timing of contractor arrival at your booth during installation is critical to avoid delays, additional expenses, or possible damage to your booth structure.

For example, if you plan to hang a large company banner from the ceiling over the center of your booth, remember that you will need to rent a scissor lift from the convention center to secure the banner. Because the lift will need to be driven into the center of your physical booth space, be sure you schedule the banner installation to occur before the booth structure is assembled.

Are you considering displaying a car or other type of vehicle in your booth? That opens a whole new set of issues that require consideration. You will need to work closely with the show decorator to determine when the vehicle can enter the hall and understand the safety requirements you must follow.

You need to know the order in which all the different elements of booth assembly and installation interconnect.

This order will ensure each group of laborers:

♦ Arrives at your space at a specific time
♦ Can begin work on time without waiting around for others to finish their job
♦ Will not damage any work already completed

As an example, suppose you reserved a 30 x 40 ft. island booth space.

♦ You created a large company sign that will hang from the convention center ceiling over the booth.
♦ You have a MINI Cooper automobile to display in the booth.

- You rented three white leather sofas and two glass coffee tables from the show contractor to include in the corner of your booth as a casual seating area.
- You need to order electrical service and hire show labor to install your booth.
- Your target move-in day and time is Tuesday from 8:00 a.m. to 6:30 p.m.

Think about all the services I just mentioned and the specific installation order.

1. First comes the company sign. The forklift and riggers need access to the booth space to hang it from the ceiling. Complete the sign installation before the booth carpet, so the forklift doesn't dirty or damage your carpet.
2. The electrical service installation comes next for computers, lighting, and other devices requiring electricity.
3. Lay down foam padding and carpet.
4. Drive the car in next before setting the rest of the materials in place. You'll need the extra booth space to more easily maneuver it into position.
5. Show labor can now install the booth structure.
6. Once booth construction is complete, placement of rented furniture comes next. The timing of the furniture's arrival after the car and booth structure is in place will give you a better idea of whether the placement you originally had in mind will work or if you need to reposition furniture to allow for better flow.

As you can see in this example, the order of installation is an important consideration.

Now, let's get back to your specific needs. Assess the services you need for your show. Separate them into those that need to be done before, during, and after your booth structure is installed. For example,

Pre-booth installation needs
♦ Hanging signage vendor
♦ Carpet installation
♦ Visqueen carpet cover
♦ Vehicles

Booth installation needs
♦ Booth structure and furniture owned by you
♦ Electrical
♦ Signage
♦ Internet
♦ Rented furniture

Post-booth installation needs
♦ Flowers/plants
♦ Carpet vacuuming
♦ Food delivery

Create your own list of show services you require.

Make sure to coordinate with each service vendor. Let them know exactly where they stand in the installation timeline and when you expect them to arrive at your booth to complete their installation. Keep each of your service providers informed of your progress and if any of your installation plans change.

Part 3
On-Site Tips

Chapter 19: Planes, Trains, and Automobiles

Team Transportation Options

If I'd only known earlier

No matter how much you plan, there always seems to be product literature or something else that needs to be shipped overnight to the hotel right before the show begins.

I have often sent an item to myself at the hotel to ensure it makes it to the show on time.

There may also be last-minute graphics that require on-site printing because there's not enough time to print it near your office and ship it 2,000 miles to the convention center. This has certainly happened to me.

When considering transportation options, it's easy to forget about items shipped to your hotel or a large graphic you need to pick up from a local printer.

If you must move boxes from your hotel to the convention center or carry an oversized poster from a print shop to your booth, you need to decide how you will get them there.

You can throw two boxes of literature into the back of an Uber or taxi, but an 8 ft. sign will not fit very well.

R equest an Uber? Hail a taxi? Rent a car? Take the subway? Hop on a bus? This decision is not as easy as you may think.

You have a wide variety of transportation options to get you around during your upcoming trade show, and there is no one size fits all answer. The transportation option you select will most likely be different for every show.

Even within your own company, different team members may require different types of transportation. Your CEO may stay close to the convention center during the show but decide to drive one hundred miles out of town to visit his parents when the show is over.

Your booth staff will be in the expo hall during the day and attending local networking parties at night. They will be near the hotel and convention center the whole time.

Your salespeople will spend time in the booth but may also travel to visit customers in the surrounding area. It's a perfect opportunity to meet in person since they've already flown halfway across the country for the show.

Your requirements and the requirements of your team will determine the transportation choices you make. The location of the show will also determine the transportation options available to you. A trade show or conference in San Diego, California, with a population of 1.42 million, will offer you every conceivable transportation option—a ride-hailing company, train, taxi, rental car, bus, pedicab, trolley, water shuttle, scooter, and more. A trade show in Carmel, California, with a population of 3,831, will have more limited transportation options.

Included in my considerations and recommendations for this chapter, I am assuming that you are traveling far enough that you will get there by plane or train. That will require you to use some of these different transportation options when you arrive.

If the show occurs in the city you are currently in, you will already know the best transportation options for your needs. If the show is within a one-hundred-mile radius of your location, you may drive yourself or carpool with other members of your team.

In-city transportation considerations

Before you select your best transportation option, there are questions to ask and considerations to make.

♦ What is the distance from the airport or train station to the convention center and hotel where you will be staying?

♦ What is the distance from your hotel to the convention center?

♦ Where are the restaurants and additional conference facilities located in relation to each other? Are they within walking distance?

♦ Is public transportation available? How late into the evening does it run?

♦ Can you quickly and easily get an Uber, Lyft, or taxi if you need one?

♦ Does your hotel have a free shuttle to the convention center or any other locations?

A small conference with five hundred attendees at the Hyatt Regency in Buffalo, New York, may only require a couple of Uber rides to get from the airport to the hotel and back again.

The Consumer Electronics Show in Las Vegas or the North American International Auto Show in Detroit, which cover multiple physical locations and welcome hundreds of thousands of attendees, will require you to visit several buildings over greater distances.

In this case, additional transportation options such as a free shuttle service between all show venues, famous sites, and restaurants around the city may be available to you.

Your transportation options

Since you are your company's trade show manager, your transportation requirements are unique.

You will most likely arrive at the show city one or two days before the rest of your team. You may also be one of the last to leave when the show is over.

Because you are arriving early and will still be running around after the show ends, it is best not to tie yourself to your other team members' transportation plans. Manage your transportation requirements first. If you can accommodate others, that's great, but be flexible in the transportation options you choose. Don't commit to sharing the cost of a car rental with two other team members before considering what you will be doing at the show.

Transportation options for your team

While you are not required to make transportation arrangements for your team, you should tell them about the transportation options available to them. You can include this as part of the package of show information you will provide to them two or three weeks before the show begins.

Give them all the logistics information for the city in which the show will take place.

- ◆ Name of the city where the show will take place
- ◆ Name and address of the hotel where your team will stay
- ◆ Name and address of the convention center where the show or conference will take place

- Distance between your hotel and the convention center or show hotel—if you are not staying at the show hotel
- Dates, times, and locations of any networking events or other activities your company is hosting, sponsoring, or has committed to attending
- Any travel your team may be required to do between the expo hall, educational sessions, and keynote presentations that may take place at different locations across the city

While giving the distance between your hotel and the convention to your team members and booth staff may seem unnecessary, you can never provide them with too much information.

Team members, especially those who have never participated in a trade show, will have many questions about when to arrive, what to do, what to expect, how to act, how to get from place to place, and so much more. Providing detailed transportation information will help them feel comfortable knowing where to go and what to do. It will also decrease the number of calls you receive at all hours of the day and night.

It's best not to dictate specific travel requirements but provide different options and let your team members select the best transportation option for each of them. If your company has a per diem for daily travel, you may want to mention the total amount paid to each employee per day for transportation expenses.

As a reminder, per diem is a standard business term for a daily allowance. It is a specific amount of money a company gives a traveling employee for expenses like hotel, food, and transportation. If your company has a transportation per diem, let your team know, so they understand upfront how much your company is willing to pay. Anything above that, the employee will need to pay on their own.

Chapter 20:
What You Don't Know Can Cost You

Understanding Drayage

If I'd only known earlier

I'll admit it. When I managed my first trade show, I thought drayage was the same as shipping. Or at least that drayage is included as part of the shipping cost.

I calculated what I expected the shipping cost to be and added it to my expense spreadsheet to make sure I stayed within budget.

At the end of the show, I received both my shipping invoice and a separate bill for the show decorator's drayage expenses. It included different line items than my shipping invoice.

To say that I was concerned is an understatement.

My shipping/drayage costs were now 25 percent higher than I had anticipated, and it put me over budget.

What was my boss going to say about this added expense? I couldn't admit that I didn't know what drayage was. That's why this chapter is so important to me. I don't want you to have the same experience.

W hen calculating your long list of trade show expenses, drayage is one of those line items that can be obscure and misunderstood. People new to trade show management sometimes believe drayage is just another word for shipping and assume it is part of the total shipping cost quoted. Both assumptions are incorrect.

It can be quite shocking and sink your budget when the show is over, and the drayage bill comes due.

Drayage primarily refers to the handling of your booth materials before, during, and after the show. This material handling expense is separate from the shipping cost you will incur to transport your booth and materials to and from the show.

Let's compare the difference between shipping expenses and drayage expenses:

Shipping expense

Shipping expenses include:

♦ The movement of your booth, collateral, signage, tchotchkes, and other materials, from your company's office or the exhibit house to the show's advance warehouse or the loading dock of the convention center, conference center, or hotel before the show begins

♦ The shipment of your materials from the show's loading dock back to your office, your exhibit house, or any other location after the show is over

Drayage expense

Drayage expenses include:

♦ Paperwork processing to allow your booth and materials to enter and leave the convention center or expo hall

- The physical movement of your booth, collateral, signage, tchotchkes, and other materials by the employees of the convention center, conference center, or hotel from the loading dock or another delivery location to your booth space before the show begins
- The movement of empty boxes and crates from your booth to the holding area or boneyard for storage during booth installation
- The delivery of any packages to your booth while the show is taking place

As an example, I once ran out of product brochures at a show in Miami, Florida. I asked my marketing coordinator back at the office to FedEx another product literature box to our booth. The FedEx driver dropped off the package at the convention center's loading dock. A person at the loading dock then took the package and brought it to our booth. In this example, the FedEx delivery is a shipping expense. The convention center employee bringing the package to your booth is the drayage expense.

Other examples include:

- The movement of the empty boxes and crates from the boneyard back to your booth when the show is over
- The movement of your packed boxes and crates from your booth space after the show back to the loading dock to be shipped to your office, exhibit house, or other location

These are just a few examples of drayage expenses that you may incur. Here is another example. I could not attend a trade show in Houston, Texas, and sent our marketing manager in my place. I provided him with drawings and photos of how the booth should look once assembled. On the morning of opening day, he sent me a picture of the booth, so proud of how great it looked. I realized that a tall vertical metal frame holding a large banner was missing and told him that the frame and banner must still be in one of the crates. Since the two crates were now in the boneyard, my marketing manager had to get the show decorator's staff to go to the boneyard, find our company's crates, open them, look for the missing pieces, and bring them to us for installation. Requesting show labor to locate parts of our booth in storage is another example of a drayage expense.

How drayage is calculated

Drayage is typically calculated based on the weight of your materials and the number of packages.

As you can see with my last example, items included in a drayage charge and the actual dollar amounts associated with them vary from show to show and city to city. That's why it's challenging to have an accurate drayage account cost before or during the show. Some expenses you will know ahead of time, and others you will not.

Weigh your materials before they are shipped. This will enable you to calculate the cost of moving your booth from the hall's loading dock to your booth space. You will know during installation how many crates you are sending to the boneyard. You can also guess the weight of post-show materials, which show labor will bring from your booth back to the loading dock. Since these are standard drayage line items that every exhibitor incurs, you can develop a ballpark rate for your budget spreadsheet.

What's unknown is whether you will need to visit the boneyard for lost items, have individual packages delivered during show hours, or have an emergency that requires the help of additional show staff. Unforeseeable events like these can add up throughout the show and increase your budgeted drayage expense by 5-25 percent, or more.

You will find a drayage or material handling form in your show's exhibitor services manual. Calculate both your expected shipping and drayage costs individually to better budget for two of your more significant expenses.

Chapter 21:
Beyond the Fishbowl

insider insight

Lead Management

The term most frequently used in the trade show business to describe the lead generation process is *lead retrieval.* Lead retrieval is often used as the umbrella term in blog posts and educational videos to explain all aspects of the lead acquisition and distribution process.

In reality, lead retrieval is just one stage of the four-stage lead management process.

1. Lead generation
2. Lead capture
3. Lead retrieval
4. Lead follow-up

The complete lead management process is a critical component of your success and should be part of your exhibitor strategy from the beginning.

It requires you to make specific decisions:

♦ What strategies are you going to use to generate leads in your booth and throughout the show? See **Lead generation stage** for examples.

♦ How will you capture those leads? Will you use standard contact form fields, or will you develop a list of custom questions to ask? A combination of standard fields and custom questions is helpful to qualify each potential lead. Write each of the questions you want your booth staff to ask.

♦ From on-site creation to sales distribution, how will you handle the leads?

♦ Will you gather all leads each day and hold on to them until the end of the show?

♦ How will you prevent leads from disappearing?

♦ Where will you put the lead retrieval devices in the evening to ensure they are secure?

♦ How will you retrieve the leads from wherever they may be and prepare them for your sales team's follow-up?

Here is an example of how your lead management plan may look:

1. Establish specific goals and objectives for your leads.
2. Develop lead generation tactics to help achieve the objectives you have created.
3. Determine how you will capture show leads.
   - Will you rent the show's badge reader?
   - Does your company have its own app?
   - Are you using old-fashioned paper and pen?
4. Create the post-show lead follow-up process and timeline.
   - How many days after the show ends will your sales team make the first phone calls?
   - Will you send automated thank you emails to everyone who stopped by your booth? The emails need to be written now and entered into your system. For example:

     Email 1
     Show end + two days = Leads are entered into the CRM system and assigned to specific salespeople.

     Email 2
     Show end + three days = Automated thank you email is sent to all contacts to thank them for spending time with you at the show.

     Email 3
     Show end + four days = Follow-up calls by sales to all assigned leads begins.

Email 4

Show end + seven days = Second round of phone calls to those leads not reached by phone during the first call.

Email 5

Show end + eight days = Automated email is sent to all leads announcing winners of the booth contest and additional call to action with urgency to encourage leads to sign up for the show promotion, which is ending soon.

5. Write a short list of specific questions that staffers will use to qualify each booth visitor.

6. Ensure you upload those questions to the badge reader, app, or other lead retrieval tool during your pre-show implementation.

7. Work with your sales team to agree on how you will distribute, and they will follow up on leads after the show is over. What will the process be? How will the reporting look?

8. During the show, monitor the collected leads to ensure qualifying questions are answered and leads captured accurately.

9. As soon as the show is over, collect and secure all leads until you can enter them into your company's CRM lead management software or marketing automation tool.

10. Make the leads available to your sales team immediately so they can follow up with emails, phone calls, and other communications previously agreed to.

Lead generation stage

What are the different ways you are going to generate leads at the show?

The following are all different ways of generating leads for your company. Even something as simple as placing a fishbowl on a table next to the aisle with a sign that reads, "Place your business card in the fishbowl to win an Amazon Echo."

♦ You will most certainly require your booth staff to speak with visitors about their needs and how your products and services help meet those needs.

♦ You may play a game or have a contest in which people will enter their contact information to win a prize.

♦ You may ask a targeted group of attendees to join you at a reception or networking event one evening.

♦ You may invite presentation attendees to stop by your booth for a special offer only available to them.

Granted, some of these examples are not the best ways to generate qualified leads, but they will generate contacts. How you choose to qualify them is up to you.

Lead capture stage

How will you capture the leads when speaking to booth visitors, holding a contest, or inviting people to an after-hours reception?

I've included here some of the most frequently used options with their benefits and drawbacks.

Lead capture options include old-fashioned paper forms, a traditional badge reader or lead capture device, a commercial smartphone or tablet app, a business card scanner, and a proprietary app your in-house IT team develops solely for your company's use. Let's get into each of them in a little more detail.

Lead retrieval stage

Now you need to retrieve the leads you collected and prepare to enter or upload them into your choice of CRM or marketing automation application. These could be Salesforce, HubSpot, or other tools with which you may already be familiar.

If you use paper leads, you should have already determined who will manually enter them into your system and how quickly they will do it.

If you used the show's lead retrieval device, it might take a few days or a week for show management to provide you with a comma-separated values (CSVs) file of all scanned badges and entered leads. You should be able to quickly and easily transfer the data directly to your CRM and marketing automation software if you use a cloud-based lead capture application on a mobile device.

Don't forget about any business cards you may have collected along the way. Those will need to be typed into your system manually or with a business card scanner.

How quickly you can transfer your leads' contact information will determine how fast your sales team can begin the follow-up process.

Lead follow-up stage

Sales scripts and automated emails should have been created and put in place as part of pre-show lead management.

Now it's time for your sales team to start dialing for dollars and for your marketing team to push send on your follow-up emails. As I've already mentioned, the call and email follow-up process, timing, and message should be agreed to, finalized, and put in place before the show even begins. You want to start closing deals as soon as you're back in the office.

So many lead capture options

Collecting new qualified leads is an essential exhibitor management responsibility and one of the top three reasons companies exhibit.

The lead capture process includes the actual device or material used, specific qualifying questions you create, and the process of capturing all leads post-show to follow up on them immediately. We should actually refer to it as lead capture, lead qualifying, and lead retrieval, in that order.

Whatever term you use, the two most critical components of this lead generation process are:

1. That you qualify as best as possible all the contacts with whom you speak. Salespeople will be quickly discouraged if you hand them 250 business cards with no notes whatsoever.

2. Once the show is over, the clock starts ticking. You should distribute and follow up on these leads immediately after the show is over. You need to reach out to them before your competitors do.

While there are many ways to capture the booth visitors' contact information, one way is not necessarily better than the rest. They each have their benefits and drawbacks. It depends on how you want to capture the leads, if you can download the leads electronically, if your CRM or marketing automation systems accept lead data in its native format, and much more. Here are a few examples.

Paper forms

Benefit: While a paper lead form may seem old school, sometimes the old ways still work just fine. A paper lead form is entirely customizable. You can make it as long or as short as you want. Since you create it from scratch, you can request any information and ask any questions you would like. There are no compatibility issues with any technology or applications you might already be using.

No internet connection is required.

Drawback: Depending on the number of leads you collect, it may take some time for all the contact information and additional data to be entered into your electronic systems back at the office after the show is over.

There is no automatic backup. If you lose the paper forms and did not make copies, they are gone forever.

Show's lead capture device or badge reader

Benefit: Since this device is rented directly from the show's official lead management contractor, its database is connected to the show's attendee and exhibitor registration lists. You will have access to much of the data each attendee entered into the system when registering for the show. Since you can download attendee data as a CSV file post-show, Microsoft Excel is a quick and easy tool for data analysis and segmentation. You can then add notes and upload the data to a wide variety of sales or marketing applications.

Drawback: Some shows will not enable you to download leads at the end of each day or even at the end of the show. They may take two to three days before giving you access to your leads via their electronic portal. This delay causes a lag in your sales team reaching out to leads who may have already been contacted by your competitor.

Renting a lead capture device at each show is also more expensive than if you use a lead capture/lead retrieval app and download it to your company or employee-owned smartphones or tablets.

Tablet or smartphone apps

Benefit: Because your mobile device is always with you, you can not only collect leads at your booth but also at a networking event, your hotel lobby, or any location with an internet connection. The data collected is immediately available to you at the show and your sales team back at the office. Salespeople can fulfill literature requests and begin the follow-up process before the show ends.

Drawback: Web-based apps require a continuous internet connection. Unfortunately, a trade show's Wi-Fi connection can be spotty, unpredictable, and slow. This unpredictability can make a web-based lead capture app a challenge to use.

When researching the best app for your needs, see if you can find one with offline capability. This online and offline ability enables you to capture leads on the device and upload the information when a strong and consistent internet connection is available.

Business card scanner

Benefit: Even if you choose to use a badge reader or a smartphone app to capture leads, your booth staff will collect a small number of business cards from visitors as well as attendees who drop their cards into a fishbowl to win a prize.

Having a business card scanner in your booth helps ensure you can scan the cards immediately, so they are not left in a salesperson's pocket or dropped to the bottom of a bag. Using a scanner also reduces transcription time and expense and enables you to distribute the contact information to your sales team more quickly for follow-up.

Drawback: Some trade show attendees choose not to carry business cards because they assume you will use a badge scanner or a web-enabled app. If your only lead capture device is a business card scanner, you will be unable to capture the contact information of attendees who don't bring cards.

Also, not all business card scanners are created equal. Some are simply scanners, only able to capture an image of the card. Others can read familiar characters and fonts but have trouble understanding script-style fonts or foreign characters. These will require additional transcription to make sure the information is correct.

Secure your leads

No matter the lead capture device or method you choose, it is critical that you secure and maintain control over your leads so your team can effectively follow up on them and close sales. These leads are your trade show's most valuable assets.

As a young, inexperienced exhibitor, I will admit that I was nonchalant about my company's leads. I left paper leads in an unlocked cabinet in our booth overnight. I allowed each salesperson to keep the business cards they collected. I waited until the show was over, and I was back at my desk before uploading leads into our CRM database for sales follow-up.

As I became more experienced and understood the implications of losing leads, I began to guard my company's leads with my life. I never put paper forms or business cards in my checked luggage for fear my suitcase will get lost and the leads will disappear. I also make backup copies of CSV or other electronic files for fear the file will be corrupted if my laptop crashes.

These measures may make me sound paranoid, but I have had these things happen, and I don't want them to happen to you.

Write effective qualifying questions that will make your sales team's job easier

The goal of successful lead capture is not simply to collect as many names as you can.

If you collect 250 contact names at a trade show but, when your sales team calls them to follow up, none of the contacts are interested in your product or service, not only will your sales team be miserable, but the return on your trade show investment will be zero.

Work closely with your sales team to create a list of qualifying questions that your booth staff can ask visitors to determine their needs, their level of interest, and how likely they are to purchase your product or service.

Regardless of your marketing tactics, you and your sales team should already have a set of criteria that you use to determine if a person is an MQL or an SQL. Use these criteria to develop the list of questions your booth staff will ask and which they will enter into your lead capture device.

Following the criteria you put in place will enable you to assess all the leads after the show and separate them into three different buckets for follow-up.

Sales qualified leads. You should immediately give your sales team the names of booth visitors who answered all the trade show questions such that they are determined to already be sales qualified leads.

Marketing qualified leads. Leads that meet all marketing criteria but not sales criteria should receive your post-show marketing communications. You may then want to include them in an ongoing nurture campaign, which will provide the lead with more information about your company and services until they become a sales qualified lead based on additional criteria they have met over time.

Unqualified leads. The trade show contacts who are not considered either marketing or sales qualified leads based on the answers they provided should be added to your database to receive ongoing electronic communication. Calling them right now would most likely be a waste of your sales team's time.

This segmentation will enable you to provide the warmest leads to your sales team for immediate follow-up and close. Nurture marketing qualified leads until they become sales qualified leads. Collect and market to unqualified leads, but don't waste your sales team's time trying to close contacts who are currently nowhere near ready to buy.

Taking time to develop targeted qualifying questions may seem like a small thing, but it can produce oversized results for the effort. A few quickly answered questions would vastly improve your ability to prioritize and follow up on leads, boosting your results and trade show ROI.

Insider insight

Keep in mind that every show is different.

Your goals and objectives will be different.

Your audience will be different.

Evaluate your lead qualifying questions before every show, enabling you to customize them for the new audience and your evolving business objectives.

A software company exhibiting at a trade show of end-user business professionals should ask questions about how the attendees use the software in their business to complete tasks, what outcomes they are looking for, and what challenges they are trying to overcome.

The same software company exhibiting at a trade show of technical professionals like system administrators and IT managers will ask questions about their requirements for software ease of installation, management, network integration, data storage, and security.

Chapter 22:
Where Is That Popcorn Smell Coming From?

insider insight

Food and Beverage Distribution

If I'd only known earlier

I was exhibiting in Seattle, Washington, and decided to order a coffee station from the show caterer for our booth. It was a bar-type setup with two coffee machines, an area for cream, sugar, stirrers, and a catering employee making coffee for our visitors.

Since we decided to include the coffee station only two weeks before the show started and our crates had already arrived at the advance warehouse, our exhibit house could not remove existing booth furniture to make space for the coffee station. Redecorating would have to be done on the fly. We no longer needed the previously ordered booth seating because the coffee station had to go in its place, with electricity rerouted to power the coffee machines.

Learn my lesson now while you are reading this book. Be sure you incorporate all elements of the booth layout while the design is still on paper. It will be much easier to ensure you have sufficient space for food and drink distribution while the design is still in development.

(continued)

(continued)
A last-minute change to the finished booth structure's layout is one element of added stress you don't need.

Today's trade show exhibitor is expanding beyond simply offering a bowl of mints, hard candies, or party-size chocolate bars.

Have you ever walked down an expo hall aisle and smelled fresh baked cookies, hot buttered popcorn, or hazelnut-flavored coffee? I certainly have. The magnificent scent pulls me by my nose through the crowds and down the aisles until I find the booth.

Once I get there, I'm no longer thinking about my sore feet or the ten-pound bag of product literature and tchotchkes I'm carrying on my shoulder. I'm thinking about getting a cup of coffee or a box of popcorn.

Of course, I don't run away after I've picked it up. I linger. I enjoy the first handful of popcorn or the first sip of coffee. I look around at the booth I'm in to see who the company is and what they do.

The few seconds I take to linger in their booth allows someone from the exhibiting company's staff to come over and introduce themselves. They've got me just where they want me. They've made me happy and content. Now it's time for them to qualify my lead potential, give me their sales pitch, and scan my badge so they can contact me in the future.

Align food with well-known cities

The food or drinks you serve to attendees and how you present it enables you to make a long-lasting impression and use it as a reminder of conversations they had with you.

While both attendees and exhibitors travel to shows to meet new prospects, generate qualified leads, and close new customers, they also like the time spent in the city where the show is taking place and want to take home a souvenir of where they've been.

Think about the city where your show is taking place and any distinguishing features of that city—like well-known landmarks or specialties unique to that location.

For example, suppose the trade show is taking place in San Francisco. In that case, you may want to create unique graphics for water bottles, coffee cups, or wine glasses with your company logo, website URL, a message or tagline that you are using at the show, and an image of a San Francisco cable car.

Boston is well-known as the home of Boston baked beans and often referred to as *Beantown*. You may want to consider handing out small ceramic bean pots with Boston Baked Bean candy inside. You can print your company name and website URL on one side of the pot and a Boston landmark like Boston Red Sox baseball's Fenway Park or the US Navy ship, USS Constitution, printed on the other side. It will be a cute souvenir of the attendees' visit to Boston. They will keep it on their desk after the candy is gone, and it will remind them of their conversation with your team.

While there are some great benefits to offering free food and drinks in your booth, there can also be some significant drawbacks if you don't follow the rules.

Don't let your food be taken away—or worse—before you hand it out

If you decide to distribute food and or drinks, you must inform the show's approved catering services company of your plans.

Your exhibitor services manual includes a catering section that discusses the rules for food distribution in your booth, if you will need to hire separate staff from the show's exclusive caterer, and how much it will cost. Read this section of the manual carefully to understand what you can and cannot do.

Realize that any exhibitor handing out food or drink is a competitor to the expo hall's food concessions and the catering department, taking away potential revenue from them by giving out complimentary refreshments to attendees. These complimentary refreshments can include *any* food and drink from small bags of peanuts or bottled water to a full bar and hors d'oeuvres.

If your company is in the food industry or is exhibiting at a food-related trade show, you can distribute a specific amount of food and drink based on the number of attendees. However, it is still essential for you to review the food services requirements to determine how much is allowed.

If you are not in the food industry, it will cost you money to distribute food and drinks in your booth. That is simply the cost of doing business and another line item you need in your trade show budget. The punishment for not coordinating with the catering team can range from a stern conversation and a small fine to your booth shut down for the show's duration.

While some exhibitors will take the chance and are willing to pay a fine if they get caught, it's not worth the hassle, embarrassment, and possibly having your booth shut down if they catch you not following the rules.

Insider insight

Cookie ovens, popcorn machines, coffee makers, and other appliances all require electricity.

(continued)

(continued)

It can be easy to overlook these items when determining how much electricity you need to order for your booth. Be sure to factor these devices into your calculation before sending the electrical services order form to the show decorator.

Chapter 23:
Your Most Loyal Fans
Current Customer Value

If I'd only known earlier

Trade show and conference participation give you the unique opportunity to interact with both prospects and current customers.

As 50 percent of your company's sales equation, existing customers are essential to market to, upsell and cross-sell to, and share some love with while you are at the show.

They are more likely to buy additional products and services on-site at the show or shortly after it is over. This condensed sales cycle enables you to drive immediate sales while waiting to close new deals with long-term prospects and new show leads.

If I asked you why your company chose to exhibit at a trade show, what would your answer be? You would most likely pick one or more of these answers.

- To generate new quality leads
- To talk to large numbers of prospects over a short period

- To validate pre-launch products with potential buyers
- To conduct competitive intelligence
- To seek out new supplier or vendor partnerships

While these reasons are undoubtedly good ones, and most other exhibitors may answer similarly, something is missing.

Take another look at these answers. Do you notice the common theme?

Each of these answers focuses on lead generation and new business development. While lead generation and new business development are important, they encompass only half of the sales equation. They are only the first element of two very distinct phases in the customer's journey.

Phase 1

The first phase occurs before they become a customer when they are a prospect, an opportunity, and a lead. The prospect will:

1. Search for a solution to a problem.
2. Create a list of supplier companies who can help them solve that problem.
3. Conduct online research.
4. Narrow the list of possible suppliers to two or three contenders.
5. Conduct more in-depth research like participating in product demos or speaking with employees at a trade show.
6. Attend a speaker session to hear from one of the company's executives.

For you, this is the first phase as well. It is the phase when you search for the prospect's details in your database, invite them to your booth at an upcoming show, ask them to join you for an informal lunch-and-learn event, and make sure they are on your email list to receive your nurture campaign.

Once you convince them of your value, they buy your product or sign your contract and become a customer.

Congratulations!

For many customers, that's where the full-court marketing press ends.

Since the prospect is now a customer, he or she becomes the sales team's responsibility, and you and your marketing team have moved on to generating new leads.

Have you ever said this out loud? Is this how you feel as a marketer? Is this the way it is in your company?

Understand that this new customer is more valuable to you now than they were as a lead.

They have entered Phase 2.

Phase 2

Phase 2 of the customer's journey is about being a customer.

As a customer, they already know your company and your team.

They trust you.

They like your products or services.

They are more open to receiving communication from you about your company and your products because they already have a relationship with you.

This customer is ripe for you to cross-sell additional products or services to them.

As a marketer, I'm sure you know the statistic that it costs less to retain an existing customer than it does to go out and find new customers. The *Harvard Business Review* estimates that acquiring a new customer can cost five to twenty-five times more than retaining a current customer. Research conducted by Frederick Reichheld of Bain & Company also concludes that even a small 5 percent increase in a company's customer retention rate increases its profits by 25-95 percent.

Think about this. While your focus on lead generation and new business development will increase the number of new customers and sales over time, it will not generate an immediate spike in revenue—which is what your senior management team wants.

So, how does this relate to your upcoming trade show? While you are focused on marketing campaigns to generate booth traffic and meetings with prospects and leads, don't forget about current customers from whom you can generate immediate interest and additional revenue.

Trade show marketing and sales for your current prospects

Take the opportunity to reach out to prospects in the city in which the show is taking place.

As part of your pre-show marketing activities, search your CRM database for prospects within a one-hundred-mile radius of the convention center.

Conduct an email campaign letting them know that you will be at the show. Give them your booth number, and provide staff names. Give them a discount registration code if you received one from the show organizer.

Include the fact that your company will be exhibiting at the show in the signature of all email communications sent out manually or from your marketing automation software like HubSpot, Marketo, Eloqua, or others. Ensure it includes the show dates, location, your company's booth number, a link to the show's registration page, and the discount code if appropriate.

For warm prospects with whom your sales team has been in close personal contact, have the appropriate salesperson reach out to set up an on-site meeting at the show.

Trade show marketing and sales for your current customers

Current customers should also receive email campaigns similar to those you will send to prospects. But be sure to keep the prospect and customer lists separate. Your prospect emails will need to remind prospects of what your company does and why they will want to visit your booth at the show.

Your current customers already know your company, so your customer emails should have a more familiar tone and remind them how much you value them. You'll want your customers to "feel the love" that your company has for them. What are some of the ways you can do that?

♦ As part of your pre-show email campaign, let them know you will be exhibiting. Give them your booth number and include the names of your booth staff and senior management who will be attending the show. Their account manager, customer care representative, or a senior executive might be attending, and the opportunity to meet them in person may give your customer the incentive to participate.

♦ If they cannot attend the show, offer to have their salesperson visit their office a day or two before or after the show takes place. Not only does this visit enable the salesperson to meet the customer in person and develop a deeper personal relationship, but since he or she has already traveled to the customer's city for the show, traveling to the customer's office to meet in person will be a negligible expense.

- Is a member of your company speaking during an educational session? Invite your customers to attend.
- Send out personal invitations to an after-hours networking reception or a customer appreciation dinner. The event will give you additional face time with customers and enable you to gain valuable insights by talking with them about your products or services, what they think your company is doing well, and what you could be doing better.

Do not ignore these opportunities to engage your current customers personally and show them how valuable they are to you.

Chapter 24: Don't Sit Down or Eat That Salad

Booth Etiquette

If I'd only known earlier

It takes a trade show attendee just a few seconds to form an impression of a company and its staff as they walk by a booth.

What will they see when they walk by your booth? A smiling person who says hello and asks them how they like the show or someone sitting in the corner of the booth with their shoes off filling their mouth with french fries?

A favorable impression may cause them to start a conversation and ultimately become a customer.

An unfavorable impression, real or imagined, will cause them to ignore you and keep on walking.

Make sure a visitor's impression of your booth staff is a good one.

This topic reminds me of times over the years when friends or family members would ask, "What's new at your job? Where are you going next?" I would tell them that I'm going to Germany for a conference, Las Vegas for a trade show, or some other far-off location for a business event. They would tell me how wonderful it sounded, wished they had my job, and asked if they could come along and carry my suitcase.

As each trade show approaches, my anticipation builds. I love going to new places, meeting new people, talking about technology-related subjects, catching up with old colleagues, and seeing customers in person who I have only chatted with over the phone or email.

As much fun as a trade show is, it can bring with it long twenty-hour days. I get up three hours before the rest of the team to make sure the schedule is in place for the day's meetings, and everyone knows where they must be at their appointed booth duty time. I respond to emails that came in overnight and get to the booth an hour before the expo hall opens to ensure that all the lights still work, a fresh supply of product literature is in place, and our carpet is clean.

Once the expo hall closes for the day, it's on to dinner with a potential client, then a networking reception, a party hosted by an important trade show sponsor, and then back to my hotel room where I check and respond to emails for another two hours before I go to bed.

While my travel may seem exciting to friends and family, they don't know how grueling and fast-paced it can be. You will have a similar experience.

The temptation to sit in one of those chairs you rented for your booth will be strong. I know what you'll say to yourself,

I'll just sit for five minutes to rest my feet, but I'll jump up if someone comes by who looks like they're interested in chatting about our products.

Back-to-back customer meetings on the show floor may also cause you to grab a salad at the food concession and bring it back to your booth to eat before the next customer arrives.

While the implications of sitting down or having a quick lunch in your booth seem small, they are not.

Please do not let anyone on your team sit down or eat lunch in full view of potential customers walking by. Whether you realize it or not, this sends absolutely the wrong message.

When these potential customers see someone sitting or eating in your booth, they are thinking:

- You are disinterested in what you are supposed to be doing.
- You are tired.
- You cannot be bothered with me—your potential customer.
- Your comfort and your stomach are more important than the job at hand.

While these impressions may be inaccurate, they are natural. They'll cause the people you are trying to attract to keep walking and never interact with you. Unless it is a separate area specifically designed for in-booth client and vendor meetings, sitting in your booth is a no-no, as is eating lunch.

I'm certainly not saying that your employees should never take a break or eat anything until the show has ended for the day—quite the contrary.

I know firsthand how exhausting a trade show can be. I have personally stood for thousands of hours on hard concrete floors at hundreds of trade shows in exhibit halls around the world. I absolutely understand how tiring a show can be.

When creating your staffing schedule, try and assign no more than four consecutive hours of booth duty per employee. If you have a 10 x 10 ft. booth at a three-day trade show, with eight hours of exhibit time, and you are sending six employees to staff your booth, this is relatively easy to accomplish.

However, most companies want to send as few employees as possible due to the hotel, food, and transportation costs, and the time spent out of the office. The larger your booth and the more limited your staff, the more difficult this will be to accomplish.

Don't forget, while your primary objective is for these people to staff your booth and generate qualified leads, you also want your team to gain an insight into other elements of the show. You can't be everywhere and see everything, so you need to use the rest of your team to be your eyes and ears.

Giving them free time throughout the day not only enables them to find a quiet place outside of the show hall to sit and relax or enjoy a casual lunch, but it also provides them with opportunities to support your scouting or information gathering efforts.

Ask a couple of your staff members to visit competitor's booths to find out what products or services they are promoting and collect any product literature they may have available.

Find out if a competitor is offering special promotions, if attendees can play a game in the booth, or if they have a contest to win special prizes.

Gathering information on what your competitors are doing will give you insights into their marketing messages and strategy and help you plan for how to position your company at next year's show.

You may also want to ask your staff to attend educational sessions of interest to your company. The materials they collect and the people they meet while they are off having lunch or completing other assignments can be just as valuable as the time they spend in your booth.

Giving them time away from the booth will also help them come back refreshed and ready to convert those trade show attendees into new customers.

Chapter 25: You Want Me to Do What!?

save money

Reserving Next Year's Booth Space Now

If I'd only known earlier

As an exhibitor, you need to make sure the trade show you select is right for your business.

♦ Does it attract the correct type of attendees?
♦ Is the expo hall open to booth visitors all day or just two hours a day?
♦ Will the show generate a lot of booth traffic, or will most attendees be at the educational presentations and never make it to your booth?

If this is your first time exhibiting, it's hard to decide whether the show will be a good return on your company's investment or not while it is still going on. But this is a decision the show's sales team is going to want you to make while you are on-site before the show is over.

They want you to make it . . . now!

It takes time to determine if the show you are currently exhibiting at was a success, if you met your goals and objectives, and if you would consider exhibiting again next year. Then why would the trade show ask you to sign up to exhibit at next year's show now before this one is over?

While your trade show or expo is still in full swing, you will receive an email in your inbox or find a paper flier in your booth from the show's sales team. It will inform you that they have scheduled a time while the show is still going on for you to meet with one of their representatives at the sales office to:

♦ Discuss where the show will take place next year.
♦ Review the floor plan and booth layouts for the convention center, conference center, or hotel they have selected to hold the event.
♦ Choose your new booth space.

You're probably thinking, *"This show isn't even over, and they want me to pick a booth for next year's show already? What's up with that?"*

There are two opposing objectives at work here.

The show's objective

From the show's perspective, this meeting enables them to tell you about their new and exciting plans for next year, lock you into a commitment to exhibit at their event one year in advance, and require you to hand over a deposit. They will position the benefits as:

♦ It enables you to select a premium booth space early before new, first-time exhibitors can reserve their space.
♦ You receive a substantial discount for booking your space so far in advance.

Although these reasons sound good, you should understand the drawbacks of committing to next year's show before this year's show is over and the financial penalties you could incur if you need to cancel.

Your exhibitor objective

The objective for you as an exhibitor is to get back to your office, decompress, speak with your team, follow up on the leads, close some deals, understand the event's ROI, and decide whether it will be worthwhile to exhibit again next year.

You don't want to be forced into anything you are not ready to do while this show is still going on.

There is a method to the meeting date and time selected for you

The sales meeting date and time assigned to each exhibitor are based on your current booth's size and the number of years you have been an exhibitor.

The company with the largest booth that has exhibited for the most years will have their meeting first.

For example, if the largest booths in the hall are two 40 x 40 ft. island booths with one company that has exhibited at the show for three years and one that has exhibited for five years, the company with the 40 x 40 ft. space that has exhibited for five years will have their meeting first. The other company exhibiting for three years will meet second.

A company that has been an exhibitor for six of the twelve years of the show but is only exhibiting in a 10 x 10 ft. booth may have their meeting scheduled for the last day. Although they are a previous exhibitor, they have always reserved the smallest booth space, so the companies with larger booths will be ahead of them.

Read the fine print

I certainly understand that you may not be ready to make a firm decision on exhibiting next year, but don't ignore the invitation to meet.

Go to the meeting. Listen to what the salesperson has to say. Just make sure that you read the contract's fine print carefully.

Cancellation policies vary from event to event, so be sure to discuss the policy with the sales representative before signing anything.

There are two types of cancellation policies:

Policy 1

This cancellation policy has a thirty-day opt-out clause, which enables you to cancel your contract up to thirty days after the current show is over without incurring any financial penalty.

Policy 2

This cancellation policy requires an up-front percentage of payment when you sign the contract. If you cancel any time after the contract is signed, you will receive X percent of your money back.

For example, if you cancel up to 152 days before the show, you will receive 80 percent of your money back. If you cancel up to 120 days before the show, you will receive 60 percent back. If you cancel up to ninety days before the show, you will receive 40 percent back. If you cancel after sixty days, you receive no money back. In this scenario, you will never receive the total amount of your money back. You will always lose some money.

What should your strategy be?

If you are sure that you want to exhibit again next year, sign up during your sales appointment at the current show to receive your booth space for the next show. You will benefit from a discounted rate, and you will be able to select from a wider variety of available booth spaces.

Be sure to study the new show's floor plan and come to the meeting with three or four booth location options in mind. If this will only be your second time exhibiting, you will most likely not receive your company's first choice of booth space. You may have to request two, three, or four options before the sales manager confirms that the space is available.

Once this year's show has ended, the sales department will open all other unreserved booth spaces to the public. If you wait until the show is over to contact the sales department, you will be competing for booth space against any other company that may choose to exhibit. This will considerably limit the size and location of the booth you can reserve.

If you are uncertain about next year's participation but can cancel without a financial penalty up to thirty days after the current show, then sign up. Just remember, add a note in your calendar or a task to your to-do list within the month after the show has ended. By this time, you should have received your final bills for the current show and better understand your total cost.

Talk with your sales team about how their follow-up calls are going with the people you met at the show. How many of them are sales qualified leads? How many have become customers? Did this show meet your company's overall goals and objectives? Discuss with your vice president of sales and your CMO about your company's exhibitor strategy for next year and if the show will still be appropriate for your go-to-market and sales growth strategies.

These questions will help you better evaluate this year's success and whether you want to exhibit again next year. If the answer is no, be sure to cancel that contract before the thirty days are up.

Part 4
Post-Show Tips

Chapter 26: I Bet I Can Get Out Faster Than You

insider insight

Booth Dismantle

If I'd only known earlier

At my first large US trade show, we had two wooden crates containing the booth structure, collateral, and giveaway items. I put the empty boxes into the crates and gave them to show labor to be placed in the boneyard for storage until the show was over.

When the show ended, I had to wait one and a half hours before the crates and boxes were delivered back to our booth and we could begin packing up.

Since then, I have kept specific boxes and other packing materials in the booth—inside cabinets, and under skirted tables. This enables me to begin packing key pieces of the booth while waiting for the rest of the crates and boxes to arrive.

It doesn't matter what industry your company is in, which trade show you are exhibiting at, or the event's size. Every trade show ends the same way. The announcement from show management comes over the expo hall's loudspeakers:

Hello everyone. Your attention, please.
Thank you for spending the last three days with us here
at [insert show name] in [insert city name].
We've had a wonderful time getting to know you, and
we hope you've learned many new things that you can
put into practice when you get back to your office.
Our conference is now over. Please have a safe trip home.
We look forward to seeing you again next year.

Even before the speaker finishes and you hear the loudspeaker click off, exhibitors begin to shove extra product literature back into empty boxes that have been hiding under draped tables for the duration of the show. The race to dismantle the booth as quickly as possible has begun.

This same scene plays itself out at every show. It takes hours or even days to set up your company's booth during installation and half that time to take it down when the show is over.

Why?

Because everyone is in a race to get out of the hall as quickly as possible to catch a plane or go sightseeing around the city before they head home.

Because of the rush to head out the door, screws, light bulbs, extension cords, graphics, and even large sections of the booth structure are lost, damaged, misplaced, and just plain forgotten.

Where your boxes and crates are dictates how quickly you can get out of the hall

When you assemble your booth during installation, you have two options for storing empty boxes and crates.

1. Show management allows you to hide boxes under a table covered by a long skirt or enclosed in any booth structure

you may have such as a product display or demo cabinet with a door. You don't want booth visitors to see empty boxes lying around.

2. If you have larger shipping containers that you cannot hide in your booth, you will need to request stickers from the show decorator, imprinted with the word EMPTY. Place the stickers on any boxes, cases, or crates that you will use at the end of the show but cannot keep in your booth. The show staff will pick up these items from the front of your booth during installation. They will store them in the show's boneyard for the event's duration.

The boneyard is an unused area of the exhibit hall set aside by show management to store exhibitors' empty boxes, crates, and other materials they do not need during the show but will need again when the show is over. It may also include extra furniture and other materials owned by the show decorator.

As soon as the show is over, the staff will begin to return boxes and crates to each exhibitor. If your crates are in the front of the boneyard, where they can be accessed and returned quickly, the time you must wait to receive them after the show is over will be minimal. If your crates are in the back of the boneyard with other exhibitor crates in front of yours, you may have to wait an hour or more before you can begin to pack up.

Insider insight

If you must stand around waiting for boxes to come back from the boneyard, don't be surprised if you encounter a delay in getting to the airport to catch your plane.

(continued)

(continued)

Think about what materials you can store in your booth so you can begin to pack up even if not all the boxes have been returned.

Do you have a product display that includes many fragile pieces and takes time to disassemble, carefully wrap, and pack? Since it will take time for the show staff to deliver your materials from the boneyard, you may want to store the bubble wrap for your product display in the booth during the show. You can wrap your display while waiting and dismantle the rest of your booth as soon as the crates and boxes arrive.

Procedure to follow if your booth returns to your office

Once you and the rest of your team return to your office and are hit with the reality of desks full of paperwork, overflowing email inboxes, and full voice mailboxes, it's easy to forget about the show.

If you had the booth shipped back to your office to be stored, the temptation is to stick all the boxes in a closet or a spare office and forget about them until a few weeks before the next show. Resist this urge.

On a Friday afternoon or a pseudo-holiday when many of your customers are unavailable, find an out-of-the-way place around your office where you can reassemble the booth and go over it with a fine-tooth comb.

♦   Is the booth damaged?
♦   Are there pieces missing?
♦   Should any of the graphics be replaced?
♦   Do table covers or other fabric pieces need to be cleaned?

The vital question to continually ask yourself is, "Could I use the booth again in its present condition at the next show? Would I be proud to have it seen by potential customers and my CEO?" Then, create a list of specific items you must replace or repair.

Procedure to follow if your booth returns to your exhibit house

If you have a custom booth built by an exhibit house, the booth will most likely be shipped back to their facility after the show. Exhibit house employees will reassemble it and take an inventory of what needs to be cleaned or replaced.

Booth reassembly, evaluation, and monthly storage are services offered by most exhibit houses for an additional charge. It is something you should discuss when evaluating companies to build your booth.

Once your booth's evaluation has finished, the exhibit house will send you a complete inventory of items requiring replacement and the cost to get the booth back into tip-top shape for the next show.

Whether the crates and boxes return to your office or exhibit house, conduct an assessment shortly after the booth returns and conditions are calmer. If you don't do it now, you will be scrambling to get it done right before the next show begins.

Chapter 27:
It's Only Over When It's Over
Post-Show Activities

If I'd only known earlier

By now, you're probably heaving a massive sigh of relief.

You started planning for your show three, six, nine, or even twelve months ago. There were so many little details to consider.

You had to select just the right show, develop an overall strategy, establish goals and objectives, and execute a plan that would deliver a successful outcome.

The day finally came when your well-appointed team welcomed eager attendees into your beautiful new booth. You enjoyed engaging in conversation with potential customers and had a great time out on the town making new friends.

You packed the boxes and sent the booth on its way back to your office or the exhibit house for storage.

You've arrived at the airport for your flight home. There's just enough time for a cold beer and a self-congratulatory pat on the back for a job well done.

Hold on a minute.

Your job isn't done!

R emember when I told you at the beginning of this book that a trade show is not simply the two, three, or four days you are physically on-site at the show?

As you are now aware, it includes the months of preparation before the show takes place. It also includes a few weeks after the last box is packed up at the end of the show when you're back at the office.

Remember, your post-show component of trade show management includes those activities that can help close qualified leads and turn them into paying customers.

Collect leads and distribute to sales

Whether your leads are in a CSV file, the cloud, on pieces of paper, or business cards, you need to collect and segment them into cold, warm, and hot leads and upload them into your CRM database for immediate sales follow-up.

This step is critical to the successful ROI of most exhibiting companies.

Implement your lead follow-up strategy

This is the follow-up to the lead management strategy you established between the sales and marketing teams as part of your pre-show activities. Begin your follow-up email campaign and sales calls, and make sure they are working smoothly.

Calculate final expenses

Throughout the pre-show and on-site phases of exhibitor management, you have received invoices and paid bills for print collateral, booth staff shirts, and many more items. You should be keeping a running total of expenses and evaluating how it aligns with your budget.

Even though the show is now over, final expenses for items like drayage, post-show booth shipment, catered food and alcohol, and hotel room charges are now coming due. While you should have a cost estimate for these items, additional charges or a credit may be applied.

You won't have the actual dollar amounts until the show decorator, your shipper, and other vendors provide you with costs.

It could take from a few days to a month for you to be able to finalize the total actual cost of your company's trade show participation.

Determine the return on your trade show investment

While a company's return on investment typically centers around the number of leads it collects, the number of leads that convert to paying customers, and the total revenue generated from those customers, a successful ROI can be different from exhibitor to exhibitor.

A significant financial return like an increase in customer sales is usually proof of a successful ROI. But you can measure success in other ways.

Suppose your objective is to obtain a large amount of press coverage for your new product launch, including interviews and feature articles in national business newspapers and trade magazines. In that case, you may determine that exhibiting enabled you to demonstrate your product to many more reporters than you would ever have been able to reach or be interviewed by if you had not exhibited.

The level to which you have achieved your original objectives will determine your return on your trade show investment.

I will discuss this in more detail in the next chapter.

Assess booth usability and take an inventory count

The booth materials have now arrived back at your office or your exhibit house. As the structure is evaluated for usability, assign someone on your team or from the exhibit house to also inventory all the nonstructural materials. This list should include the amount of product literature, giveaway items, lead capture devices, office supplies, extension cords, pens, and cleaning rags that have returned from the show.

Now is the time to determine which materials need replacing. Things like extension cords and cleaning supplies can be purchased immediately and stored with the booth, so you don't have to worry about them before the next show.

Look closely at your product literature and determine if it can be reordered and used for the next show or if it will need to be redesigned with new marketing messages to make it appropriate for a new audience.

Similarly, evaluate your water bottles and other giveaway items to determine if you should place a new order or if another type of swag will be more appropriate for the next show. Collateral and giveaway items take time to produce, so counting the numbers you currently have in stock and placing a new order well in advance of the next show will ensure that you do not pay rush charges on printing and shipping.

Survey your team

While you have your impressions on how the show went, each member of your booth staff has had their own experience.

They were on the front lines, actively speaking with show attendees. They know what marketing and sales messages resonated with visitors, which giveaway items were popular, and if you had actively engaged visitors at your demo station. Survey each of them on their booth experience.

Don't forget to survey your executive team and other employees who may have attended the show but did not spend time in your booth. They had a different show experience. They participated in a keynote presentation, had lunch with other attendees, and met with potential vendor partners.

You can request participant insights and thoughts by asking them to complete a survey online, in an email, in a Word document, or even on a piece of paper. It doesn't have to be fancy or formal. Your team will appreciate that you are interested in their honest assessment and will be happy to provide you with their comments.

Build a master trade show database

Evaluate all the elements of show management that made it a success or helped make your job easier.

♦ Were there resources, people, or other factors you can use in the future?

♦ Did you find a fantastic promotional products company that can turn trade show shirt orders around very quickly to accommodate additional staff participation? You'll want to keep their order information handy for the next show.

♦ Did the shipping company's driver get you out of a tight jam, going above and beyond to get the booth to the hall within your target time? Save his contact information so you can request that he be your truck driver for the next show.

Create a master trade show database of information, materials, people, and resources you want to use when preparing for future shows. This central hub will help you, your staff, and anyone who joins your team to have one location for go-to trade show resources you know you can count on over and over again.

Chapter 28: Saying It Was Good, Isn't Good Enough

insider insight

Total Return on Investment

(continued)
allocate marketing funds to trade shows was if I had hard facts to back up my weak explanation. Never again did I complete a trade show without evaluating its return on investment.

R OI can be a funny thing. As a marketer for thirty years, I can remember when we manually created spreadsheets to track a campaign's success or verbally asked a salesperson which leads became customers and which did not. Oh. Wait a minute. That wasn't thirty years ago. Some companies are still doing that today. Is your company still working that way?

Hearing one of your salespeople say they had good conversations with booth visitors is not enough to determine that your trade show was a success.

As we've already discussed, there are different reasons why companies exhibit at trade shows.

To establish a presence in a new industry.

To solidify a leadership position among competitors.

To generate more leads.

To sign up more customers.

Whatever the reason, it is essential that you objectively evaluate whether the show was a financial success and if it helped you achieve your business goals. That is what your executive management team will want to know.

Insider insight

When calculating a show's financial return, be sure to include travel expenses, drayage, and additional costs that you will not

(continued)

(continued)
know until after the show is over. The addition of these expenses will help ensure that you have an accurate and complete view of all expenses and can subtract it from the new revenue generated to determine the show's profitability.

Additional insider insight

Calculating the financial return on how many new customers you have secured because of a trade show is easy.

Figuring the return on other objectives may produce a less immediate financial return but can be just as important in moving a lead from prospect to customer.

For example, you may have a 15 percent increase in online eBook downloads because of a unique offer code you provided to show attendees. You may have a 20 percent increase in newsletter signups because of the post-show *thank you for stopping by our booth* email you sent to all booth visitors.

While these actions cannot immediately demonstrate a financial return, they are marketing metrics that should be monitored and tracked to determine how many eventually become customers.

As I discuss further in chapter 29, you should ideally create a comprehensive show report, which evaluates the success of the show by providing answers to some of these questions:

♦ What were your business objectives and corporate goals for the show? Were they met? If not, why?
♦ How many leads did you receive?

- How many of these could be considered potential direct customers or resellers?
- Are any of these current customers?
- Are any of these former customers who are interested in becoming customers again?
- How many do you categorize as MQLs, SQLs, or simply contacts to be included in your ongoing nurture campaign?

♦ What is your cost per lead? Determine this by dividing all show costs by the total number of qualified leads.

♦ Did you receive any free media as a result of the show?
- Did you close any new customers because of the coverage?
- What was the value of these sales?

♦ Did you conduct a pre-show marketing campaign to invite attendees to visit your booth?
- How many pieces did you distribute?
- What was the cost?
- How many attendees visited the booth as a result?

While it can be challenging to calculate an actual return, marketing automation tools and the integration between sales and marketing technologies make the analytics portion of our job easier every year. Show analysis is key to whether your return on investment is successful.

Now, let's create a report based on your company's requirements. I will give you a few elements you should include, and you can add some of your own as you get inspiration from my examples.

Be honest with your assessment. Identify the positive outcomes as well as the areas for improvement when conveying the event's value. Here we go.

Chapter 29:
So, How Did It Go?

Post-Show Analysis and Reporting

If I'd only known earlier

You know the old saying: "If a tree falls in the woods and no one's around to hear it, does it make a sound?"

I have a new saying: "If you exhibit at a trade show and you don't analyze the outcome, was it a success?"

I'm always tempted to simply move on to the next task as soon as a show is over.

My voice mailbox is full of messages.

My inbox is full of emails.

This show is over, and the next show is coming up in four months. I need to focus on the next one now.

No! I need to fight the urge and finish what I started.

And you do too.

You planned for this show for months. You arrived at the hall before the rest of your team to ensure booth installation went smoothly. You returned to your hotel room each evening after dinner and a networking event to work long into the night.

You stood on a hard cement floor—even with extra deep padding under the carpet—in your booth for hours on end over four days.

You were the last to leave the hall at the end of the show after everything was packed and shipping paperwork completed.

If you haven't experienced this because you have yet to complete your first trade show, get ready. You will experience it.

If you have experienced it, I completely understand what you're going through. The show is over. Finally! You want to move on to the next project and put this show behind you. I get it.

The reality is that, like every other marketing campaign or program you implement, you must assess the success of your participation and report on the outcome to your company's executives and stakeholders.

The campaigns proven successful have more money allocated to them, and you will do more of them. Less successful campaigns are tweaked to make them more successful, or you eliminate them and use the money for another activity.

A best practice is to evaluate the success of your individual event programs and campaigns at each stage along the way—pre-show, on-site, and post-show. Now that the show is over, it's time to report on the results. Not simply on what went well and what you could do differently, but hard numbers such as an actual budget vs. estimated budget comparison, total leads vs. sales qualified leads, estimated ROI vs. actual ROI, and so on.

As I already discussed in chapter 3, on average, 20-25 percent of a company's marketing budget is set aside for trade shows. That is a large percentage of the budget for a single marketing channel. However, if you attend the right show, with the right audience, you have the right message, and your participation is a success, your CMO, CFO, and CEO may:

- Happily increase your budget to do more of the same
- Instruct you to transfer existing funds from less successful campaigns to increase your trade show participation

If your last show was not a success, you might choose to:

- Not exhibit at the same show next year
- Adjust your strategy for the next show
- Reduce your participation in shows altogether and reallocate the funds to other marketing channels

You will never know which way you should turn if you don't analyze and report whether a show has met your company's goals and objectives.

How long should the report be?

I know you're asking, "How long should this report be?"

The answer is, "As long as it needs to be to provide a comprehensive assessment of the results of your exhibitor efforts." It could be four pages, eight pages, or more.

There is no recommended length. The length of the report is up to you. The contents and size will be determined based on the requirements of your company's stakeholders.

A large, multipage document containing detailed descriptions of booth activities, individual sales meetings set, and the number of press interviews secured is appropriate for your CMO and sales VP.

Your CEO may request a two-page summary of essential data such as lead-to-customer conversions and actual ROI.

Timing of a comprehensive report

On the one hand, you want to create your report while many of the show's nuances are fresh in your mind. On the other hand, you may not have received the final show expenses like shipping and drayage, so you're unable to do an expected vs. actual budget comparison.

Your products may also have a long sales cycle, and it can take months to determine the number of new customers who have come on board because of the show.

Your management team will be interested in receiving your report as quickly as possible. If this is the case in your organization, you may want to create a preliminary report including all the data you already have, with a note that you will follow up in a couple of weeks or a month or two with the final, detailed report.

Elements of a comprehensive report

There are many elements you can include in a comprehensive report. I have included some below. I'm sure you can think of even more that are of specific importance to you.

Executive summary

The executive summary is always the report's first section. It is a one- or two-page overview of the outcome of your company's participation. It includes a synopsis of the information the reader will find at greater length throughout the report. For example:

- Original objectives
- Lead quality
- Potential revenue
- Number of press interviews and articles published
- Show assessment
- Emerging trends
- Estimated budget vs. actual spend

Goals and objectives

The whole point of this report is to determine if you have met the goals and objectives you first established months ago during your pre-show planning. This section should include a brief recap of those objectives. The following sections of the report will help determine if you achieved the appropriate return on your objectives.

Lead generation, sales conversion, potential revenue, and net new revenue generated

Lead generation is just the first step on the way to new customers and an increase in company revenue. This section should include:

♦ The total number of leads received
♦ The total number of marketing and sales qualified leads
♦ A breakdown of the number of leads into hot, warm, and cold to determine the likelihood and time frame to close
♦ The cost per lead

Sales opportunities, revenue generated

This includes:

♦ The number of new customers acquired as of the completion of the report (i.e., net new customers)
♦ Actual sales revenue already realized from new customers (i.e., revenue generated from new customers)
♦ Potential revenue from new customers (i.e., sales opportunity from new customers)
♦ Actual cross-sell revenue already realized from existing customers (i.e., revenue generated from current customers)
♦ Potential cross-sell revenue from existing customers (i.e., sales opportunity from current customers)

Meetings held

♦ The number of on-site meetings held with current customers

♦ The number of on-site meetings held with potential customers or leads

♦ The number of meetings scheduled and held post-show

Press and analyst coverage

While it can be challenging to directly tie an interview with a reporter or an article about your new product launch with an X percent increase in sales and an X percent increase in revenue, quantifying the number of interviews, articles written, and other media efforts can help you evaluate how effective your media outreach is in generating new leads and increasing brand awareness. You can include:

♦ How many company press kits, in print or online, were downloaded or taken by any media members?

♦ Which members of the media attended your speaker session? Which publications or websites do they represent? How many reached out after the presentation for follow-up conversations or interviews?

♦ If you distributed a press release, how many times was the announcement published or reposted, and what media outlets were they—magazines, television stations, websites, newspapers?

♦ How many articles were written based on what the journalist, reporter, or blogger learned about your company and products at the show?

• In which publications or websites were the articles?

- What is the readership circulation number for each publication?
♦ How many interviews did you conduct with reporters, journalists, or bloggers at the show?
  - What was the subject of each discussion, i.e., was the focus corporate or product-based?
  - Which members of your company participated in the interviews?
  - What publication or website did the reporters represent?
  - Were any commitments made to write and publish an article based on the interviews?

Exhibit value (booth efficiency and effectiveness)

Assess all booth elements to determine what worked well, what you should do more of in the future, and what needs to be changed to increase its effectiveness.

Booth structure

♦ Was the booth easy to install and dismantle?
♦ How long did it take to install and dismantle, and how many people were required to do this?
♦ Did the materials used in the booth, like orange laminate countertops and ivory-colored imitation leather sofas, stand up to high booth traffic? Were they easily damaged? Did they get dirty quickly?
♦ Can the booth be used again, or will a large percentage of the structure need to be refurbished?

Booth layout

♦ Were the layout and flow of the booth inviting to people?

- Did it encourage interaction between booth staff and attendees?
- Was the booth size large enough to accomplish all objectives you had for the show?
- Was the booth located in the right area of the hall to attract the most traffic?

Product focus
- If you displayed several different products, which ones were of most interest to visitors?

Demos
- If you conducted product demos in the booth, which demos were most popular with visitors?
- How many total booth visitors did you have? How many of those visitors took the time to watch a demo?

Graphics
- Did passersby quickly and easily understand the messaging?
- Did the look and feel, messaging, graphics, and colors work well together to present a cohesive booth?

Marketing effectiveness: pre-show, on-site, post-show
Just as you do for any marketing campaign, determine your pre-show, on-site, and post-show marketing results. These may include:

- The number of email invitations and announcements sent to the show's preregistered list
- The number of pre-show appointments set
- The number of leads who became customers using the unique show code you provided to booth visitors

- The number of new leads at your evening reception or networking event

Booth staff effectiveness

- Were the correct variety of staff members in the booth at any given time? (i.e., sales expertise vs. product expertise vs. technical expertise)
- Did the staff receive the proper pre-show training?
- How effective was each staff member in explaining your core messages and competitive position to booth visitors?
- What are the results of the post-show staff survey?

Return on objectives

Way back in chapter 1, I mentioned that a goal is a wish, but an objective is quantifiable. An objective helps you determine how close you have come to reaching your goal.

Write down the objectives you initially selected for this show and include the final numbers you achieved. For example:

- If your objective was to speak with thirty booth visitors per day, did you actually talk with that number of people? Was it more or less?
- If you aimed to conduct fifty product demos throughout the show, how many did you perform?

Budget comparison

What was your original budget estimate for this show?

- How did the forecast for booth components, sales materials, show labor, shipping, drayage, exhibitor services, staffing, transportation, hotel, marketing campaigns, and additional expenses break down?

♦ How did those initial estimates compare to actual post-show figures?

♦ After reviewing all show expenses, did your costs come in under budget, at budget, or over budget?

♦ Were there any areas of the budget that came in considerably over or under the original estimate? Should they be adjusted for the next show? For example, if you estimated that your shipping cost would be $2,000 and the final price was $4,000, you should reassess how you calculate your shipping budget for the next show.

Competitive review

♦ Which of your competitors exhibited at the show?

♦ What was their booth size and location in the hall?

♦ What are your thoughts on their booth traffic, contests, games, visitor engagement, and other activities taking place in their booth?

♦ What was their product focus? What were their key messages?

♦ Did you pick up corporate brochures, product collateral, or other materials from your competitors' booths? (Note: if so, let your team and executive management know that these materials are available for review.)

♦ What marketing did they do?
- Did they purchase a sponsorship?
- Did they advertise in the show guide?
- Did they distribute a press release?
- Did they speak during the educational sessions?

- Did they conduct an email campaign to the preregistered list?

Show assessment

When you initially decided to exhibit at this show, you most likely read the exhibitor brochure or prospectus. It included information like the number of expected attendees, attendee demographics, and their areas of interest.

Now that the show is over, do your post-show impressions match what you understood the show would be about and the audience it would attract?

- Were the actual attendees the same as those described in the exhibitor prospectus, or were they different than you expected?
- Did the educational speaker session topics help in generating the type of attendees that are important to you?
- Were the attendee demographics as described or different?
  - For example, were there more international attendees than you were led to believe?
  - Were there a larger number of women than men?
- Were any new marketing strategies used to promote the show to a new group of potential attendees?
- Were virtual attendees able to participate as well?
  - How were exhibitors able to engage with these attendees?
  - Were the lead generation efforts you used to engage virtual attendees successful?
- Did show management select the proper city in which to hold the show? Did exhibiting in this city help you reach more of your target audience?

Educational speaker sessions

If a team member spoke at the show, be sure to include information on their presentation results. If no one from your team spoke, it is still important to provide your assessment of the educational sessions to determine if you should submit a speaker request for next year's show and what topics will be of interest to the attendees.

♦ If a member of your team spoke:
  • How many seats were available in the room?
  • How many people attended the presentation?
  • How many people stayed in the room afterward to talk personally with your speaker?
  • How many people who participated in the speaker session stopped by the booth to chat further?
  • How many people made a post-show appointment?
  • How many became customers?
♦ In general, what was the focus of the education sessions?
♦ What topics were of most interest to all attendees?

Conclusions and recommendations

Based on all the data and insights you collected and compiled, what are your conclusions or recommendations?
♦ What did you do well?
♦ What would you do differently? Either doing more of it or less of it.
♦ Would you exhibit at the show again next year?
♦ Would you have a bigger booth, a smaller booth, or the same size?
♦ Would you select a space in another area of the hall?
♦ Would you exhibit in your own booth or partner with a vendor for whom you resell products?

- Was your booth staff adequate? Should they be trained differently, or were they trained well? Did they have a good variety of expertise and knowledge to answer the types of questions asked?
- What are some new ideas you may want to implement at next year's show?

This comprehensive report should be created and made available to your primary stakeholders, such as your CMO and other executives who have requested a detailed account of the show's objectives and outcomes.

While your CMO will read your report from cover to cover, your CEO and CFO may simply be interested in the strategy you implemented and the results you achieved. In most cases, that means how many net new customers you acquired and the total revenue you generated.

As I mentioned in the previous chapter, the show's objective is not always to achieve an immediate financial outcome. It may be to build a new indirect reseller channel, in which case your report would include the names of the companies that have signed contracts with you, a description of their size, sales structure, product portfolio, market reach, and target customers.

No matter what information you include in the executive overview, you want to get to the point quickly. Your CEO, CFO, and others want to know that you spent the money wisely and achieved your objective.

Elements of an executive overview

Since you already created your comprehensive analysis report, you have all the information you need and can pare down the details to create an executive overview.

Your company CEO, CFO, and other members of your executive management team are most likely not interested in all the details that you include in the comprehensive trade show report. They don't have time to review a long document. They just want to know how successful the show was in helping the business achieve its goals and if you stayed on budget.

This executive overview should be no more than two pages and provide the following facts:

♦ **Goals and objectives:** What were the company's goals and objectives that you all agreed to before the show?

♦ **Outcome:** Did you meet those goals and objectives? Yes? No? By how much were you above or below your objectives?

♦ **Proposed budget vs. actual spend:** Did you spend more or less than initially proposed, or were you on budget?

♦ **How do you plan to improve and meet your goals at future shows:** List these briefly as key bullet points.

These four categories should encompass the high-level sections of your overview.

You may also want to include items like the number and quality of leads you received and the number of net new customers you have already closed.

While this chapter provides you with a large amount of suggested information that will be of interest to yourself and your CMO, it is a foundation on which you can add additional information that is uniquely important to your company.

There is no standard reporting template that we all use. When creating your report, begin with the information I included here and expand or condense as needed.

Your stakeholders and management will also tell you what information they want to see and what information is not particularly important. You may determine that the number of press interviews is of no interest to your CEO. Still, he or she will most likely want to receive more detail on the number and type of leads you received, what geography they are in, and the sales forecast for each of those leads over the next six months.

The report's value comes in gathering and assessing the data and information important to your team. It is not only valuable as a post-show assessment but provides you with renewed insights when you are trying to determine if you will exhibit the following year.

Part 5

When Your Trade Show Gets Turned Upside Down

Chapter 30:
Staying on Track Without Going Insane

Exhibitor Management in Uncertain Times

If I'd only known earlier

I have never seen such uncertainty over the status of in-person events as we experienced in 2020 and continued to experience in 2021.

It was a time the trade show industry could never have imagined in their wildest dreams, and no exhibit manager will ever forget.

The Covid-19 pandemic caused a complete shutdown of in-person trade shows and conferences starting in April 2020, and it has continued for over a year.

Some show organizers moved their in-person events from spring/summer 2020 to a virtual event in fall/winter of 2020.

Others canceled their 2020 in-person event altogether, informing potential attendees that "we'll continue to assess the in-person trade show landscape in 2021 and provide you with a new show date when we can."

You should know that, as an exhibitor, you can still stay on track executing your plans even as show dates remain uncertain.

A s a result of this titanic shift in trade show operations and what seems to be the new normal for exhibiting companies during a pandemic, exhibitor managers ask me two primary questions.

- ◆ Are live, in-person events dead?
- ◆ How can I effectively prepare to exhibit at a show when its management is uncertain about when they will reschedule their event, if it will be in-person, if it will be virtual, or if it will be a combination of both?

Here are the answers to these questions.

Are live, in-person events dead?

Certainly not. Live, in-person events are not dead. Humans are social beings and need the personal interaction that a face-to-face event provides.

However, we cannot ignore that the Covid-19 pandemic turned the trade show, conference, and exhibition market on its head.

So, what is the future of trade shows? While cities will open their convention centers again, how we execute trade shows moving forward—live in-person, virtual, or hybrid—will take a couple more years to flesh out. Until convention centers adopt uniform cleaning standards, best practices, and social distancing measures across the industry, attendees and exhibitors will not be entirely confident that business is back to normal.

I know what you're asking . . .

How can I effectively prepare to exhibit at a show when show management is uncertain about almost everything?

The short answer is, you can prepare to exhibit at shows even if you don't currently know the actual event date or the complete show management plan. How?

As an exhibitor, you know that events, whether smaller regional conferences or large industry expos, take a lot of time and effort to prepare for, so you need to start early.

On the other hand, you don't want to waste money unnecessarily, building a large trade show booth structure or creating materials you may not use.

While there is still uncertainty about what direction many upcoming trade shows will take, there are important marketing tactics that you can complete, whether your show is in-person, virtual, or a combination of both.

For example, every exhibitor produces a product flier, company brochure, or other collateral to distribute to attendees. You will need to write and design this brochure regardless of whether you ultimately print copies to distribute in person or make electronic PDF files available online.

Preparing the brochure file now and putting it aside until show management makes a final decision about what type of event will occur will eliminate the need to scramble to create the brochure from scratch when the decision is finally made.

Here are six marketing tactics that you can begin to implement immediately. If you analyze your own exhibitor checklist, I bet you will find more items to add to this list.

1. Determine how you should incorporate your company's business objectives into your trade show sales messages, collateral, and product positioning.
2. Establish specific, quantifiable objectives you want to reach, whether the show is online, in-person, or hybrid.

3. Write and design product and company brochures as well as any other necessary collateral. Hold off on printing them for now.

4. Write and create pre-show email marketing campaigns to inform prospects and customers that you will be exhibiting. Offer them a discount registration code if you have one.

5. Write and create post-show email marketing campaigns to thank participants for attending and provide them with additional information on your company and products.

6. Work with your sales team to determine what constitutes a qualified lead and agree on how the leads will be turned over to sales for immediate follow-up after the show.

   • How and when will the leads be distributed to each salesperson?

   • What will the follow-up process be, and how will the sales team convert these leads from prospect to customer?

Remember what brought you to this point

Have you already signed an agreement, committing your company to exhibit at an upcoming trade show? In an uncertain time, you will inevitably question whether you did the right thing.

Step back and remember why you decided to exhibit at the show in the first place. Maybe the attendees are your perfect target audience and having them all in one place at one time will help increase your sales exponentially. Perhaps you're launching a new product, and the show will help generate a lot of excitement for your business across your industry.

While the show management's strategy may be uncertain, your company's business objectives, which caused you to move forward in the first place, are solid. They were the right objectives aligned to the right show when you made the decision initially, and they are still the right ones now.

Although we can't eliminate the stress and anxiety over an uncertain trade show landscape, there are many activities you can complete well ahead of a final decision, the show date, and the type of event. Completing them now will help pave the way for a much smoother event season for you and your team.

Part 6
Essential Terms You Should Know

Chapter 31: What Is She Talking About?

Dictionary of Terms

If I'd only known earlier

When I first started out managing trade show exhibits, the terms people used in conversation were like a foreign language.

Bill of lading
Force majeure
Gang box
Visqueen

I tried to guess what they meant based on the conversation I was having or the sentence I was reading.

I didn't know what drayage was. While I looked it up in the exhibitor services manual, I didn't take the time to understand what it meant entirely. I simply assumed that it was part of the shipping cost.

I was incredibly shocked when the drayage bill came due after the show, and I learned what drayage really was. I also hoped

(continued)

(continued)
my boss would not fire me because this lack of knowledge had caused us to go over budget by $2,500.

That's why this chapter is so important to me. I didn't want to stick it in this book as an afterthought. I don't want you to have to experience the same worry I felt.

An author often sticks a dictionary or glossary of terms in the appendix at the back of a book as an easy way to increase the book's page count. You will notice that I gave this dictionary of terms its own chapter, chapter 31. It's that important to me, and I know it will be a valuable resource for you.

A

a/v resources. Audiovisual materials and supporting resources used during the show, including TV and computer monitors, flat panel displays, DVD players, projectors, microphones, videos, music, and other recorded sounds.

abstract. A written summary of speeches, presentations, or other educational sessions presented at the trade show. It is generally a maximum of five hundred words and describes what the presentation will be about and what the attendees should expect to learn.

accessible storage. Space maintained by the show contractor and located away from the exhibit booths. It is made available to exhibitors who have materials that will not fit in their booths but must be easily accessible at any time during the show. Items typically stored in accessible storage include brochures, promotional merchandise, and other materials to be given away to show attendees.

actual weight. Actual weight is the accurate shipping weight of all items. You can calculate the weight by weighing each freight item individually or by weighing an empty truck or shipping container, loading the truck or shipping container with all the materials, and reweighing the truck or container again to get a total weight. Subtract the smaller number from the larger number and that number will be the actual weight.

adjoining rooms. At least two rooms that share a common wall but have their own door.

advance order. An order for products or services sent to the show decorator and other contractors before the show takes place. Items may include furniture, carpet, electricity, audiovisual equipment, and plants. Pre-show order deadlines are set by the show contractor and include discounts for advance order placement and payments.

advance price. The price of an item ordered and paid for before the advance order due date. As an example, booth carpet ordered at the advanced price—before the advance order deadline—may cost $300, but for an order placed just a few days before the show, long after the advance order deadline has passed, the price may be $550.

advance warehouse. A location, usually a warehouse or similar facility, selected by show management where exhibitor shipments of freight will be received and stored prior to the show's start date. Freight can often be stored there up to thirty days before the show begins. Shortly before the scheduled move-in date and time, all items are transferred to the actual show location.

aisle carpet. The carpet laid in the aisles between booths where show attendees will walk. This carpet is one of the last items to be installed before the show begins. It is put in place by the show decorator or show contractor.

aisle signs. Signs suspended from the ceiling that hang over the public aisles and indicate each aisle's number or letter. These signs aid trade show attendees in finding exhibitor booths more quickly and easily.

ata carnet. Admission Temporaire—Temporary Admission. A customs document for the international import and export of product samples, equipment, and other items used for trade shows, conferences, and expos. It enables temporary duty-free and tax-free shipment of these goods for up to one year.

B

bandwidth. The amount of data that can be transmitted and received per second.

bare booth. Booth space only. It does not include any services, utilities, or booth structure. An exhibitor must purchase all services, furniture, utilities, and other items separately. When you sign an exhibitor contract with a trade show's management team, you are reserving and required to pay for a bare booth. The cost to build your booth, ship it, install it, dismantle it, print graphics, order electricity, rent furniture, and all other materials and services needed to exhibit are extra.

bill of lading (B/L). The document that must be completed to ship freight from one location to another. It is a contractual agreement between the shipper—whether the exhibitor or an exhibit house—and the transportation company. It includes a list of all containers, contents, weight, dimensions, and cost.

billing weight. The billing weight is used by air freight and van line providers to determine the number upon which their freight charges will be based. The billing weight is the actual weight or the dimensional weight, whichever is larger.

boneyard. An unused area of the exhibit hall set aside by show management for the storage of exhibitors' empty boxes, crates, and other materials not used during the show, but which will be needed again once the show is over. It may also include extra furniture and other materials owned by the show decorator.

booth area. The physical amount of floor space paid for by an exhibitor. The dimensions are usually sold in 10 x 10 ft. increments.

booth frontage. The measurement across the front of the booth space. For example, in a 10 x 20 ft. booth, the length across the booth's front is 20 ft., and the depth is 10 ft.

booth installation contractor. The company selected by an exhibitor to manage the people who install and dismantle the exhibitor's booth. This company may be a third-party contractor like the exhibit house that originally designed and built the booth. The booth installation contractor can also be the official show contractor if the exhibitor has hired them to install their booth.

booth number. The number assigned to each booth space. These numbers are used by show management in the expo hall's floor plan and show guide to quickly identify the floor location and exhibitor. It is also used by exhibitors in their promotional materials to invite attendees to their booth.

booth personnel. Exhibitor staff who are assigned to work in their booth. They may be employees of the exhibiting company and any third-party talent they have hired specifically for the show.

booth sign. A small cardboard sign that includes an exhibitor's name and booth number. It is used primarily to help the exhibitor find their space during installation.

booth size. The physical area of floor space rented by each exhibitor. The dimensions are usually sold in 10 x 10 ft. increments.

break-out rooms. Function rooms used for individual educational sessions held during the trade show or conference. These rooms are smaller than the large spaces used for general sessions or keynote presentations.

break-out sessions. Small presentations, panel discussions, workshops, or other sessions on specific topics of interest to a subset of attendees. They are separate from the general sessions or keynote presentations that a much larger group of participants attends.

building rules. Rules and regulations set by building management—whether convention center, hotel, or other—related to their property and included in the exhibitor services manual.

C

call for papers. An invitation by show management to submit educational topic ideas for the trade show's presentation sessions. Submission and topic requirements are made available on the show's website and referred to as a call for papers, a call for presentations, or a call for speakers. An abstract, including an overview of what the speaker will discuss and what attendees should expect to learn, will need to be completed by the proposed speaker, submitted, and evaluated by a review committee.

carrier. A transportation company that moves exhibitor freight over land, sea, or air. They often consolidate the materials of several exhibitors into one shipment bound for the same show.

certificate of insurance. Proof of insurance issued by an exhibitor's insurance provider. All exhibiting companies are required by show management to provide evidence of insurance. The amount of general liability insurance usually needed is $1 million.

cherry picker. Equipment used to lift a person or people to a specific height.

classroom setup. The arrangement of a meeting room with long rows of tables and chairs facing forward, so all participants have an area to write or use a laptop, tablet, or another device.

clean bill of lading. A receipt issued by the carrier stating that they received the contents of the shipment in good condition. See also Foul Bill of Lading for comparison.

clear date/time. The last date/time in which an exhibitor-appointed shipping carrier is required to be in line at the trade show facility's loading dock so that its truck can be loaded after the show has ended.

collection and consolidation service. A shipping company service in which several smaller shipments are picked up or received from different exhibitors and combined into one truckload. The smaller loads are then forwarded to the show as one large shipment.

co-location. Holding two or more distinct yet related conferences, trade shows, or other events at the same time in the same location.

column. A large physical pillar erected to support the weight of the building's roof or other structures over the trade show hall. Multiple pillars are located throughout the hall and may be next to an aisle or in an exhibitor's booth. It is common for them to be shown on an exhibitor floor plan as a solid square.

commercial invoice. A detailed list of shipped goods.

congress centre. A term used primarily outside of the United States to reference a large facility that holds trade shows, conferences, expositions, and other events.

consignee. The person or company to whom items are shipped.

consignor. The person or company sending freight to a destination.

contractor. A person or company that provides materials or services to a trade show and its exhibitors. They may be the official contractor hired by show management or an exhibitor-appointed contractor. Services may include booth installation, carpet, plant, or furniture rental, electrical or internet connections, drayage, etc.

corkage. An additional charge for alcoholic beverages purchased off-site and brought into an exhibitor's booth for distribution. The cost may also include items like glasses, ice, blenders, or other ancillary items.

corner booth. Exhibit space at the end of a row of inline booths, which has two sides open to aisles. A corner booth's size is typically 10 x 10 ft. or 10 x 20 ft.

crating list. A detailed list of all contents contained in a crate. Items may include graphics, lighting, literature, and booth panels.

cross aisle. A small aisle perpendicular to a central aisle in the exhibit hall. It may appear as if it is splitting a long linear or inline row of booths in half.

custom carpet. An upgrade to the standard carpet an exhibitor can order from the show decorator. It usually includes a heavier pile, possibly thicker padding underneath, and comes in a variety of specialty colors.

custom exhibit. A booth designed and constructed based on an exhibitor's exact requirements. Because it is custom, it is purchased rather than rented. It is usually built, stored, and shipped by an exhibit house or display builder for the exhibitor and likely requires professional installation and dismantling.

cut-off date (hotel). The date on which a hotel will release all unsold sleeping rooms which, up until this date, have been held as a block for trade show attendees to reserve. Once released, the rooms will be made available to the public.

cut-off time. A specific time of day in which exhibit hall contractors and union labor will stop their loading or unloading activities for the day.

cwt. Centum weight or hundredweight. A measurement of weight used when shipping trade show freight. Equal to one hundred pounds. Drayage is calculated using this measurement.

D

dead time. The time when a union worker is unable to do their work due to circumstances beyond their control.

declared value. The dollar value of the contents of the shipment as stated by the shipper.

decorator. Also known as the show contractor, the show decorator is the company hired by show management to install and dismantle booths, hall decorations, and other materials for the show and its exhibitors. Decorator services can include booth setup, pipe and drape installation, carpet, and signage completed by carpenters, painters, and other professionals as required.

direct to show shipping. Any exhibitor shipments that are sent directly to the show location—whether it be a convention center, hotel, or other location—rather than the pre-show advance warehouse.

dismantle. The teardown, packing, and shipping of all booth materials from the exhibitor's location after the trade show has ended.

display builder. Also referred to as an exhibit house or a trade show booth builder, a display builder is an independent company that designs and builds booths for exhibitors. They create custom booths for purchase but may also rent standard booth structures and design and print custom graphics.

double-decker booth. A trade show booth with multiple levels. In this case, a two-story exhibit. Often, the second level is used for private client and prospect meetings.

double time labor. Work performed beyond straight time and overtime. It is paid at twice the straight time rate. For example, if the straight time rate is $15 per hour, the double time rate would be $30 per hour.

drayage. Trade show drayage refers to the handling of exhibitor materials before, during, and after the show. It can include the movement of materials from the loading dock to the exhibitor's booth space before the show and back again afterward, the delivery of packages during the show, and storage of empty boxes during the show. This expense is in addition to the shipping costs incurred to get freight to and from the show. Also known as material handling.

E

electrical contractor. The company hired by show management to provide electrical services to each exhibitor.

empty sticker. A sticker placed on empty crates and boxes that are moved to storage before the trade show begins. The sticker includes the exhibiting company's name and booth number so show labor can return the crates and boxes to the company's booth after the show is over.

end cap booth. Also referred to as a peninsula booth, this booth space has an aisle on three sides. The fourth side abuts another exhibitor or two exhibitors.

exclusive contractor. The company selected by show management to provide labor, products, and services to all exhibitors. Two well-known general contracting companies are Freeman and GES, among many others. They are different from the exhibitor appointed contractor hired by the individual exhibitor. Also referred to as the general contractor, show decorator, or official contractor.

exclusive use. The use of a carrier's whole cargo area by one shipper.

exhibit house. Also referred to as a display builder. The company that designs and builds custom trade show booths for exhibitors. They may also rent smaller booths and design and sell custom graphics.

exhibitor appointed contractor. A contractor hired explicitly by an exhibitor to work for them before, during, or after the show. They are unrelated to any contractors retained by show management. Also referred to as an independent contractor. An exhibitor intending to use an exhibitor appointed contractor must notify and receive approval from the show decorator before booth installation can begin.

exhibitor move-in/move-out. The time exhibitors have to install their booth and prepare their space before the show begins. The time exhibitors have to dismantle and remove their booth and other materials following the show's close.

exhibitor services manual. The trade show bible for all exhibitors. It is a manual—hard copy or pdf—of everything an exhibitor needs to know about the show, including move-in and move-out times and dates, order forms for all equipment and services like furniture, electrical, decorating, and labor, as well as deadlines for all activities, rules and regulations, marketing opportunities, and everything else about an exhibitor's show participation. Also referred to as an exhibitor manual or an exhibitor services kit.

F

floor manager. A person who works for show management and is responsible for helping exhibitors during the setup and teardown of their booths and general supervision of the show floor.

floor marking. The convention center's actual marking of the expo hall floor with tape, chalk, or another material to outline the edge of each booth space. Each exhibitor's carpet, booth structure, and signs must be placed within their booth's parameters, which the tape or chalk has marked out.

floor order. An order for goods or services placed by the exhibitor on the expo hall's floor once booth setup has begun. Contrast this with an advance order, which is placed before show setup begins.

floor plan. A scale drawing usually showing the expo floor, the layout of all proposed booths, structural elements such as building columns, electrical drops, and other hall features. A floor plan may also be created for a smaller space such as a hotel, including conference rooms, ballrooms, and other event spaces.

floor port. A box recessed into the floor of each booth space containing plumbing, electrical, or telephone connections for exhibitors.

force majeure. Legal language usually found in an exhibitor contract that refers to an *Act of God* such as a tornado, earthquake, flood, or other extreme weather condition or natural disaster, which, if it occurs, could make the trade show or conference impossible or impractical to operate. This clause eliminates any legal responsibilities from the show organizer or the exhibitor.

foreman. The lead worker who manages other workers on a specific project. The foreman may work for the show contractor or the exhibitor appointed contractor.

foul bill of lading. A receipt issued by the carrier stating that the contents of the shipment were damaged when received. Contrast this with a clean bill of lading.

four-hour call. The minimum amount of time for which the exhibitor must pay union labor.

freight desk. The area of the show floor set aside to handle inbound and outbound exhibitor materials and paperwork.

freight forwarder. An independent third-party provider of shipping logistics. They manage freight movement but do not operate any planes, trucks, ships, or other vehicles. The exhibitor may hire them to manage the pickup of the exhibitor's trade show booth and other materials from an exhibit house or the exhibitor's office and ensure the shipment reaches the expo hall, hotel, or other destination in the time required.

frontage. The measurement across the front of a booth space. For example, in a 10 x 20 ft. booth, the length across the booth's front is 20 ft., and the depth is 10 ft. In a 10 x 10 ft. booth, the frontage is the same length as the booth's depth. Also referred to as front space.

G

gang box. A box containing every tool or supply that an exhibitor could need before and during the show. It may include things like extension cords, network cables, scissors, stapler, staples, a box of pens, Velcro, Scotch tape and shipping tape, measuring tape, screwdriver, paper towels, cleaning liquid, hand sanitizer, tissues, stain remover, extra batteries and light bulbs, spare keys, and so much more.

general service contractor. The company selected to provide labor, products, and services to show management and all exhibitors. Two well-known general contracting companies are Freeman and GES, among many others.

green room. A room used for keynote and general session speakers or special guests to rest, prepare for their speaker session, and enjoy refreshments.

H

hand carriable. Any items one person can carry unassisted, into and out of the expo hall. Carts or other wheeled devices cannot be used.

hand truck. Also known as a two-wheeler, dolly, or small cart, it is a two- or four-wheeled device used to transport small loads of boxes and other materials to and from your booth.

hospitality suite. A room or suite of rooms rented by an exhibitor to entertain customers, prospects, and vendors for meetings or business networking purposes. The room may be rented in the convention center, official show hotel, or another hotel in the convention center's vicinity.

housing bureau. A separate organization that provides hotel reservation services for exhibitors, speakers, and attendees.

I

infringement. An exhibitor's unlawful use of floor space outside of their assigned physical booth area. Examples include placing signs, furniture, and other materials in the public aisles.

in-house. The term used to describe services performed by a company's employees rather than being outsourced to an independent third-party business or contractor.

inline booth. A booth located in a straight line alongside several other booths in an aisle. The booth will have only one side open to the aisle—except for a corner booth—and is generally 10 x 10 ft. or 10 x 20 ft. in size. Also referred to as a linear booth.

installation and dismantle. The setup and takedown of a trade show booth. The installation and dismantle requirements vary from show to show, so be sure to read the exhibitor services manual closely for every show.

installation contractor. The company selected by the exhibitor to manage the people who install and dismantle your booth. This company may be a third-party contractor like the exhibit house that originally designed and built the booth or the official show contractor.

island booth. A booth space open to the aisles on all four sides. An island is a larger booth space starting at 20 x 20 ft. and increasing from there.

J

jigging. Custom dividers and protective padding used inside exhibit crates to prevent booth components from damage or shifting during shipping.

junction box. A metal or plastic enclosure used to house electrical wire connections. It enables electrical power to be dispersed to multiple locations.

K

kiosk. A small, freestanding structure used to display products, distribute promotional materials, conduct a demo, show a video, or other activity.

L

labor desk. Location on the show floor where exhibitors can reserve labor to help them with various activities that need to be completed.

lanyard. A fabric cord worn around the neck of all show attendees and exhibitors used to hold their name badge.

lead retrieval. A system by which an exhibitor captures contact details like the name, company name, email address, title, and other pertinent information on trade show attendees who visit their booth or interact with the exhibitor in some way. This information was traditionally captured on paper but is now most commonly captured using an electronic device. In most cases, the lead retrieval device scans the attendee's name badge to capture the stored data. It enables all data to be collected and downloaded in a standard way.

lead tracking. Whether online or offline, manual or automated, a lead tracking system collects and stores attendee contact information when visiting an exhibitor's booth. It also enables sales to follow up with them once the show is over.

linear booth. A booth space located in a straight line alongside several other booths in an aisle. The booth will have only one side open to the aisle—except for a corner booth—and is generally 10 x 10 ft. or 10 x 20 ft. in size. Also referred to as an inline booth.

M

marshaling yard. A parking lot, freight yard, or other location where all trucks carrying exhibitor freight are required to check in and wait their turn to be called to the show facility's dock for unloading. This process ensures the shipment is delivered to the hall in an orderly way and there are no roadblocks or traffic jams around the convention center or hotel.

material handling. Material handling refers to the handling of your materials before, during, and after the show. It can include movement of your items from the advance warehouse to the convention center's loading dock, from the loading dock to your booth before the show and back again after the show, delivery of packages during the show, and storage of your empty crates and boxes during the show. This expense is in addition to the shipping costs you will incur to get your freight to and from the show. Also known as drayage.

media kit. Also known as a press kit, a media kit is a collection of information provided to members of the press attending the trade show. An exhibitor media kit could include their booth number, a new product announcement, a speaker biography, a product brochure, a company backgrounder, and other informative company and product information.

media office. The trade show's on-site location where members of the media, including reporters, bloggers, photographers, journalists, and others, can collect information, conduct interviews, and write or distribute articles. Also referred to as a media room.

modular exhibit. A booth consisting of several individual pieces that an exhibitor can use together or separately depending on the required size or configuration.

move-in. The date selected by show management when exhibitors can begin to install their booths. Depending on the size of a booth or any special requirements, the move-in date can vary from one exhibitor to another.

move-out. The date selected by show management when all booths must be dismantled and shipped out of the hall.

N

net weight. The weight of all goods, excluding the shipping container.

no freight aisle. An aisle that must be kept clear of crates, boxes, trash, and all other materials during show setup and teardown. This aisle is used to deliver materials, take away empty containers, and an emergency means of egress.

O

official contractor. The company hired by show management to provide services such as booth setup and teardown, material handling, hang signs, move boxes from the loading dock to the exhibit booth, and other activities.

on consumption. The term used to describe the amount of food or beverages used by a group. The organizer will pay for the exact number of pieces of food or drink consumed.

on-site pricing. The price to order goods and services from the show decorator on the show floor. This price is higher than placing an advance order. For example, the price to rent booth carpet before the advance order deadline may be $300, but if ordered on-site during show setup, the cost could increase to $450.

outbound material handling form. An agreement between an exhibitor and transportation company to ship exhibitor freight out of the hall after the show. This document contains an inventory of the goods to be shipped, the number of boxes or crates, and the weight.

overtime labor. Work performed outside of the regular business hours, usually 8:00 a.m.–5:00 p.m., Monday through Friday. Work outside of those times is billed at a higher rate.

P

packing list. A list containing a description and quantity of each item included in a shipment.

pallet wrap. The process of using clear plastic to wrap several individual boxes onto a pallet. It enables all packages to be sent as one shipment.

pavilion. A set of adjoining booths in a specific area of the hall that have some commonality. The associated exhibitors may offer similar products, belong to a single industry, or appeal to a similar audience. For example, an automotive pavilion may include companies that produce products sold to automotive manufacturers like Ford, Mercedes Benz, Toyota, etc. A trade show with many international exhibitors and attendees may have region or country-specific pavilions like a Southeast Asian pavilion or a USA pavilion.

peninsula booth. Booth space that is open to aisles on three sides. The fourth side is next to another booth. A peninsula booth is also referred to as an end cap booth.

per diem. The daily allowance a company will pay their employees for food, lodging, transportation, and other incidental expenses.

perimeter booth. A booth space located along the outermost wall of the exhibit hall.

pipe and drape. The metal tubing (pipe) and hanging fabric (drape) used to delineate the back wall and side rails of each booth's space. The pipe and drape used for the back wall of a booth are usually 8 ft. tall. The pipe and drape for side rails between booths are traditionally 3 ft. tall.

pop-up booth. A relatively lightweight trade show display that can easily be set up and dismantled by one or two people without using a scissor lift or other heavy equipment. All pieces, including graphics, lighting, and the booth structure, can be packed into small reusable plastic cases often shipped via UPS or FedEx. It can also be brought to the airport by a company's trade show manager and sent to the show as luggage. Also known as a portable exhibit.

preferred carrier. A shipping carrier designated by the show's management as their carrier of choice.

press kit. A collection of marketing materials, including press releases, company overviews, product or service announcements, executive bios, customer success stories, and other documents made available to the show's media. These can be made available in hard copy format and dropped off in the assigned press room or made available online if an electronic press room is created for exhibitors to upload their materials. Also referred to as a media kit.

press office. Also known as the media office, the press office is the public relations or media agency location that collects and distributes trade show information to all media outlets, both print and online, interested in reporting news from the show.

press officer. The chief public relations contact in charge of the distribution of all news related to the show.

press release. A document written by the exhibitor and distributed to the media for publication. It may announce company changes, new product or service offerings, special show promotions, or other company-related news.

press room. A separate room or area of the hall set aside expressly for the media, including reporters, bloggers, and other traditional and not so traditional journalists. They may use the room to conduct interviews with exhibitors and write stories. Traditionally, the press room was also where exhibitors could drop off press kits or press releases for distribution to the media. Today, many trade shows offer a virtual press room.

Q

quad box. Four electrical outlets in one box.

R

refundable deposit. An initial monetary payment made to the show organizer or a vendor or supplier which can be returned to the exhibitor under specific circumstances agreed to by both parties.

release form. The form completed by an exhibitor to allow booth materials to be removed from the exhibit hall post-show.

retention rate. As it relates to a conference or trade show, the retention rate is the percentage of exhibitors and attendees that return to the trade show from one year to the next.

return on investment (ROI). Comparing how much revenue the trade show generated for a company vs. all associated costs they incurred for attending and exhibiting is their return on investment.

return on objectives. Comparing the actual benefits received from trade show participation vs. the original objectives determined before the event occurs is the return on objectives.

rigger. A union worker skilled at securing overhead objects, including signage, banners, lighting, temporary walls, and other booth items from the hall's ceiling.

rigging. The overhead suspension of objects from the hall's ceiling, including signage, banners, lighting, temporary walls, and other items.

room block. The total number of sleeping rooms set aside by show management for exhibitors and attendees to reserve.

S

scissor lift. A piece of equipment used to hoist a person or people into the air. A scissor lift is often used to hang show signs or exhibitor banners from the expo hall ceiling.

security cage. A portable cage that can safely store items while the trade show takes place.

security contractor. The company hired by event management to protect the expo hall and all other common areas of the trade show. An individual exhibitor can also employ them to secure their booth when the expo hall is closed.

service desk. The area in the hall where exhibitors can inquire about purchasing products and services offered by the show decorator and other vendors. These may include electricity, furniture rental, internet connectivity, decorating services, and more.

shipping case. A reusable case used to ship show materials. They are often vertical, round, or oblong plastic containers.

shipping crate. A large wooden container constructed and used to transport a trade show booth and other materials. It is rigid enough to use for multiple shows. The booth is commonly stored in the crate when not in use.

show daily. A publication, printed or electronic, produced on-site each day of the show. It features articles about exhibitors, their products or services, educational sessions, and other interesting show news.

show guide/show directory. The guide or directory is a listing of the show's who, what, where, and when. It is distributed to all exhibitors and attendees. It includes information such as the list of exhibitors and their booth numbers, a schedule of events, times and descriptions of educational speaker sessions, evening activities, and other pertinent information about the show.

show manager. Also referred to as show management. It is the company that puts on the show, contracts for space, hires the general contractor, signs exhibitors, determines presentation topics, invites speakers, promotes the event, and more.

show office. The on-site trade show or expo management team office.

show within a show. A trade show using its own name and educational tracks that takes place as part of a larger show with a similar or complementary focus.

side rail. A low wall made of metal pipe and fabric draping used to divide one booth space from another. Also known as a rail.

skirting. The fabric that is attached around the sides of tables and counters and hangs to the floor. It is often pleated and comes in a variety of colors. The hidden area under the table can be used to store boxes or materials that visitors to the booth should not see but need to be accessed quickly.

special handling. Shipments that require extra time, equipment, or labor to deliver to an exhibitor's booth. The exhibitor will incur additional fees.

sponsor/sponsorship. A sponsor is an organization or company that provides financial backing for a trade show to take place. Sponsorships are tiered marketing opportunities. Sponsorship packages may include upgrades to a larger booth space, a speaking opportunity, free passes to both the expo and educational sessions, free public relations, the complete attendee list, logo branding opportunities, and more.

staging area. An area in or near the expo hall where service providers or third-party vendors receive and review orders and assign jobs before dispatching workers or delivering items to an exhibitor's booth.

steward. The manager in charge of all hall union labor. He/she also ensures that the exhibitors follow all the show rules set out in the exhibitor services manual.

straight time labor. Work performed during regular business hours as specified by show management in the exhibitor services manual. Usually between 8:00 a.m. and 5:00 p.m., Monday through Friday. It is billed at the standard rate.

T

tabletop display. A small, modular exhibit built to stand on top of a single table or another similar surface.

talent. People hired by an exhibitor to work for them in their booth. They are not employees of the exhibiting firm. The talent may welcome visitors, entertain, demonstrate products, distribute literature, or conduct other activities.

target date. The move-in date provided to an exhibitor. This date can vary between exhibitors depending on the size of the booth and the complexity of installation.

tear down. The dismantling of all booths and other exhibit materials after the show ends.

tchotchke. Also referred to as promotional materials, giveaway items, or swag, a tchotchke is an item handed out to attendees during the show. Tchotchkes can include inexpensive items like plastic pens or reusable bags given to all attendees. They may also include expensive items only given to a select group of booth visitors who show a high level of interest in the exhibitor's products or set up a post-show meeting.

theater setup. An area within a booth set up with rows of seats theater style and used to conduct presentations or demonstrations to several attendees at one time.

third-party vendor. Any company, excluding the official show decorator, hired specifically by an exhibitor to perform tasks or provide services, including booth setup and teardown.

time and materials (T&M). How services are billed. The exhibitor is charged for the materials used and the time it takes labor to complete a task.

traffic flow. How trade show attendees move throughout an expo hall or an individual booth.

truss. A metal structure of interconnecting steel bars used to suspend lighting or other equipment. An exhibitor may also use a truss system as part of a booth structure to reduce its weight and, as a result, the shipping costs.

turnkey booth. A linear booth containing all materials needed to participate as an exhibitor, including carpet, signage, electricity, and furniture. An exhibitor can reserve a turnkey booth for a flat rate using one order form.

V

variable costs. Costs that vary based on the number of show attendees. Items with a variable cost could include tchotchkes, product brochures, and drinks.

virtual press room. A trade show's web page or area of their website focused on press and media-related topics and materials for editors, journalists, and other media professionals. Exhibitors can post company press releases, product photographs, and media alerts to the page for journalists to review at their convenience. Also referred to as a virtual press office.

virtual trade show. A trade show or conference produced electronically and presented online. Attendees can watch speaker presentations and interact with exhibitors using their computers. Live, in-person trade show organizers may also offer their participants the ability to participate in some sessions via their computer.

Visqueen. A brand name for heavy-duty plastic sheeting which covers a booth's carpet. It protects the carpet from damage and dirt due to equipment and personnel walking and rolling over it during installation. The plastic is removed shortly before the show begins.

W

waybill. An official shipping document used as a receipt showing the shipper has accepted the shipment and is now responsible for getting the shipment to its destination.

work rules. The legal rules that regulate union labor's working arrangements. They include the minimum number of hours paid, mealtimes, which jobs an exhibitor can perform on their own and which jobs must be completed by union labor, when overtime pay begins, and more.

work time. Work time is the actual time between when union labor is given to an exhibitor to work and when they are told they can leave by the exhibitor. The laborer may or may not do work during this time, but because they are assigned to the exhibitor, the exhibitor is charged for the time. For example, if a piece of the booth is missing and the workers must stand around not doing any work while the exhibitor finds the piece, the exhibitor will still be billed for this time.

Z

zero-based budgeting. A means of budgeting where all expenses must be justified and approved for each new period. In a trade show environment, zero-based budgeting refers to the fact that an exhibitor starts over with a zero budget for each new trade show. They analyze each show's requirements, goals, and expenses individually and allocate funds based on that show without referring to the needs, goals, or costs of any previous show.

Share Your Thoughts
Please Consider Writing a Review

D id you find this book helpful? If so, I'd love to hear about it. Honest reviews help readers find the right book for their needs. It would be great to be able to share this book with other trade show exhibitor managers, marketing professionals, and small business owners who could benefit from its insights and information.

Please consider posting a review on Amazon.com or wherever you purchased this book.

Thank you for your support.

Acknowledgments
Thank you

I dislike the acknowledgments section of most books. Probably because authors often use it to congratulate themselves for the terrific job they've done or to explain the book's division of labor.

It also reminds me of a movie award acceptance speech. Instead of thanking a casting director for taking a chance on a young, starving actor, who became a break-out star, it might say,

I'd like to thank my husband for putting up with me writing every morning for three hours as you raced around the kitchen to get our children breakfast.

I thought of eliminating this book's acknowledgment section but readers, particularly readers of nonfiction, expect to see it, often reading it first.

Why do I have an aversion to this section of the book? Probably because I am an introvert at heart, keeping my relationships personal and valuing their private nature. That's not to say that I do not appreciate the support I have received during the writing and publishing of this book—indeed, throughout my career.

Quite the contrary.

The foundation of this book was built on a thirty-year marketing career. It is a compilation of my experiences both good and bad, what others have taught me, what I have learned from failure and success, and what I have experienced.

I have developed personal relationships and close friendships with many business colleagues, bosses, entrepreneurs, and tech industry executives, some going back ten, twenty, and even thirty years. There are too many to mention here. I fear any list I include would be incomplete and I would insult some through unintentional omission.

So, I say thank you to those who have crossed my path throughout my journey.

Thank you to business colleagues with whom I have stayed in close contact over the years and who have become good friends.

Thank you to bosses who showed me the way and shared their expertise without hesitation.

Thank you to tech industry leaders, successful entrepreneurs, and business role models who have provided advice and made introductions, without expecting anything in return. They all know who they are.

I value our relationships and cherish the knowledge, insight, and experiences they have so willingly shared with me.

I thank them for their generosity of spirit, their knowledge, and their friendship. I am forever grateful.

It is now my turn to pay it forward.

About the Author

Lisa M. Masiello

L isa M. Masiello is an award-winning business-to-business marketing strategist and advisor to the IT industry where she has run marketing departments for fast-growing startups and leading technology providers over the past three decades.

She has personally planned, directed, attended, and exhibited at hundreds of trade shows across the United States and in countries around the world.

Lisa understands firsthand the challenges and roadblocks that trade show managers and small business owners face when preparing to exhibit. It is her mission to eliminate those challenges that can pop up unexpectedly and provide real-world insights so your journey will not only be smooth but successful.

Lisa firmly believes in generously sharing her expertise and insights. She publishes articles on business development and marketing strategy for various online publications and speaks at technology conferences on topics such as competitive differentiation, reseller channel sales, go-to-market planning, and modern marketing techniques.

Lisa loves traveling to far off locations, so when she's not learning about new technologies or writing books, you will find her studying a map and deciding where to go next. Lisa lives and works in New Hampshire, USA.

Learn more about Lisa at https://www.lisamasiello.com.

Connect with Lisa on LinkedIn at https://www.linkedin.com/in/lisamasiello.

Made in the USA
Middletown, DE
08 October 2022

12222443R00163